38

YOU
CAN
CONQUER
GRIEF
BEFORE
IT CONQUERS
YOU

YOU CAN CONQUER GRIEF BEFORE IT CONQUERS YOU

BY
LESTER SUMRALL

THOMAS NELSON PUBLISHERS
Nashville

Published in Nashville, Tennessee, by Thomas Nelson, Inc., Publishers and distributed in Canada by Lawson Falle, Ltd., Cambridge, Ontario.

Printed in the United States of America.

All Scripture quotations unless otherwise noted are from the King James Version of the Bible.

All Scripture quotations marked NKJB–NT are from the New King James Bible–New Testament, © 1979 Thomas Nelson, Inc., Publishers, Nashville, Tennessee.

The excerpt on page 74 is from *God's Trombones* by James Weldon Johnson. Copyright 1927 by The Viking Press, Inc., © renewed 1955 by Grace Nail Johnson. Reprinted by permission of Viking Penguin Inc.

Library of Congress Cataloging in Publication Data
Sumrall, Lester Frank, 1913-
   You can conquer grief before it conquers you.

   1. Grief.   2. Consolation.   I. Title.
BV4905.2.S85   248.8'6   81-13018
ISBN 0-8407-5776-X   AACR2

CONTENTS

YOU
CAN
CONQUER
GRIEF
BEFORE
IT CONQUERS
YOU

1

FIVE MEN
AND A FUNERAL

"Thirty seconds to air time!"

The director's voice crackled over the intercom in our studio at WHME-TV in South Bend, Indiana. Beyond the blinding lights, I could dimly see the sweep-hand of a clock moving toward 8:00 A.M. It was Friday, September 28, 1979.

"Tape to speed. Audio up." We could hear the musical theme introducing the program. A hush fell across the audience. A cue light on one of the color cameras winked on.

"Good morning, ladies and gentlemen," I said. "Welcome to our telethon for WHME. 'This is the day that the Lord hath made,' and we expect great blessings from the Lord as we extend the work of His kingdom through this telecast. . . ."

I did not know it, but at that very moment five of my dearest friends and co-workers lay in a soybean field near I-69, on the north side of Indianapolis. Their mangled, blood-soaked bodies were strewn across the field in the debris of their private plane.

The text for the message that morning was Mark 15:31— "Likewise also the chief priests mocking said among themselves with the scribes, He saved others; himself he cannot save." I explained to the TV audience that sacrifice is often necessary to carry out the will of God. Jesus' critics were exactly right: If He hoped to save mankind from sin, He could not save Himself from the Cross. He had to bleed and die to accomplish God's plan of redemption.

"Our generation is looking for bargain basement salvation," I said. "Sure, we would like to see millions of sinners saved; we would like to see all the heathen nations come to the Lord. But to bring this worldwide revival we're only willing to give our tips, gratuities, and freewill offerings. There is little sacrifice involved. There is no blood shed."

City patrolmen studied their maps, trying to see where the plane might have gone down. The Indianapolis tower had lost radar contact at 1:22 A.M. Perhaps the plane's transponder had gone awry. Perhaps the plane had landed somewhere else. . . .

"You know, friends," I continued, "this generation will not even give God its junk. Dresser drawers and strong boxes in the banks are full of Christians' old jewelry, old coins, stamps, heirlooms, stocks, and bonds that could be used to save our world—but this generation has refused to use them for that. The great, rich denominations of our land and the wealthiest Christians are not willing to give God more than a token of their love.

"The truth is, we cannot save this generation any more cheaply than Christ saved the human race. He had to *die* to save us!

"The apostle Paul could not transform Asia and Europe without enduring jail sentences, stonings, beatings, shipwrecks, and the deep hatred directed against him. This is why his life continues to challenge us today.

"Jesus said, 'If any man will come after me, let him deny himself, and take up his cross daily, and follow me' (Luke 9:23).

"This principle of world evangelism cannot change," I said. "Until we as Christians are willing to deny ourselves, we cannot lead this generation to Jesus Christ. Until we are willing to take up our cross—not just a little gold cross worn around the neck in remembrance of Christ, but our own burdensome cross—we cannot bring salvation to our world. Until we are willing to walk in the bloody, sacrificial footsteps of the Savior and be like Him, we cannot produce the great harvest of immortal souls that He must have in this generation."

It was one of the most thrilling days I have ever known in broadcast evangelism. People called in from many outlying cities and towns, asking how they could be saved and offering to support the work of Christian television. My mind drifted back over the many struggles we had faced since purchasing our first TV station at Indianapolis in 1972, and I silently thanked God for the people who had made this ministry possible.

I thought of Dick Crittenden, a very successful insurance executive who had helped me negotiate the purchase of the station and had given very generously to this ministry. He labored tirelessly as a host on our daily interview program, "Today with Lester Sumrall," and at the telethons on our TV stations in Miami, South Bend, and Indianapolis. Dick had a sharp mind and was a candid counselor. How often I leaned on this vibrant, forty-eight-year-old man for wisdom and support!

I thought of Ron Bayer, an energetic young man who had also helped me with the purchase of the Indianapolis station, WHMB. Just two months before, Ron had become general manager of WHMB. His lively spirit already permeated the place, inspiring the staff with a zeal for the ministry that was sure to make the work grow. Ron was only thirty-three, the same age as Jesus when He met His awful death on the cross.

Then there was John Harris, a prosperous Indiana farmer. John was ill with diabetes, nursing a large ulcer on the bottom of his foot, when I first met him. But God healed him and filled him with the Holy Spirit, then gave John an amazing way of witnessing to the unsaved. I had seen John lead scores of people to Christ as he shared his testimony on television, in prison, in church meetings, and in cottage prayer groups. John carried his Bible with him everywhere he went, and he never missed an opportunity to tell someone about Jesus. He was only forty-three years old. Surely the Lord had a great ministry ahead for him.

After delivering the message, I gathered up my notes and started to walk off the set. It was 10:00 A.M.

"Dr. Sumrall," a staff member said nervously, "the brothers who were on the platform with you last night . . . their plane is lost. They haven't arrived in Indianapolis."

That would be Dick, Ron, John, and their traveling companions, Don Jones and David Harris, John's son. A shiver ran up my spine.

Several of my staff workers were already trying to reach the Federal Aviation Administration, the state police, and any other authorities who might have word about the search. We learned that a woman had just spotted the wreckage of a light plane near the interstate, not far from the junction of Lantern Road and 106th Street. The city police thought this was where our men had gone down.

My wife, son Frank, and I got into our car and hurried south to Indianapolis. My soul was so deeply troubled that I prayed constantly as we drove.

To be honest, I didn't believe our men really had crashed. I knew they were on an errand for the Lord's work. They had left South Bend for our station in Indianapolis, still damp with the sweat of the telethon here. They were men with a God-given mission. As my friend Jerry Falwell has often said, God never permits a man to die until he has fulfilled his mission. That's how I felt about these five men. I knew John was a skillful pilot. Even in an emergency, he would know what to do. But for the sake of their wives, I felt duty-bound to be on the scene.

Over the two long hours that it took to drive to Indianapolis, I had plenty of time to meditate upon the deep Christian commitment of these men. They were truly my brothers in the Lord. I refused to think that they might be dead.

I asked God for comfort from His Word, and I felt Him leading me to Job 1:21,22, the words of Job just after he had suffered the sudden tragic loss of all his children and possessions. The Word said, "Naked came I out of my mother's womb, and naked shall I return thither: the LORD gave, and the LORD hath taken away; blessed be the name of the LORD. In all this Job sinned not, nor charged God foolishly."

Then God directed me to Job 2:9,10. There Job and his wife consider what to do in the face of their great sorrow: "Then said his wife unto him, Dost thou still retain thine integrity? curse God, and die. But he said unto her, Thou speakest as one of the foolish women speaketh. What? shall we receive good at the hand of God, and shall we not receive evil? In all this did not Job sin with his lips."

Through these verses, God reminded me that He has a life plan for every human being. God had a life plan for Job, even though Job did not know all the details of that plan. Job's wife did not know the plan; she certainly had no idea of the spiritual warfare that was raging between God and Satan over the integrity of her husband. Job's three friends did not know the plan; they could not understand why God allowed him to accept his suffering with peace of mind. He said, "Naked came I out of my mother's womb, and naked shall I return thither: the LORD gave, and the LORD hath taken away; blessed be the name of the LORD" (1:21).

In his sorrow, Job did not make foolish accusations against God. He did not sin with his lips. Suddenly I realized that, no matter how I felt about this plane crash, I must be very careful about what I said. God did not blame me for the tragedy, but He would hold me personally responsible for how I reacted to it.

Several patrol cars were parked at the side of the road when we arrived. The bodies had already been taken away.

There were no survivors.

The plane had been smashed into thousands of pieces. Even after sifting through the wreckage, Federal Aviation Agency investigators were unable to explain why the plane had crashed. The sky had been clear, with visibility of seven miles or more, and the plane still had fuel in its tanks. But for some reason, it had hit the ground at full speed, its right wingtip dragging the soil and turning the craft in a crazy cartwheel across the field.

With my son Frank and our friend Bob Montgomery, I went to the morgue in Noblesville to identify the bodies. The caskets could not be opened for showing at the funeral.

GRIEF—BUT VICTORY

When I phoned the widows, they greeted me with love and warmth. Each one said something like, "Oh, Brother Sumrall! How my husband loved you and the work you are doing! You were such an inspiration to his life!"

I was amazed. To their families and to the public, they displayed a courage not often seen. They took control of the funeral arrangements and showed their friends what it means to be a Christian victor in the hour of death. Their attitude was like that of Bonnie J. DeMott, who lost her pastor husband to leukemia seventeen months after they were married. "I do not know why God took him from me," Mrs. DeMott said, "but I believe that He will someday make the reason plain."[1] The widows of my friends held that same confident trust in their Lord. Their courage was a marvelous thing to see.

I had expected to comfort them, but they comforted me much more. God knew I needed their comfort! The moment I saw the mangled bodies of my friends there in that morgue, I was seized by an anguish unlike anything I'd ever known before. I felt my legs go limp. I gripped Frank's arm and said, "My God, my God! It's them! My God, help me!"

No words can express what a person feels at a moment like that. I was crushed. I was sick at heart.

For many days after that, I was overcome with sudden waves of sorrow. I remember preaching at our church in South Bend and breaking down in tears. Even during our television broadcasts, I began to weep uncontrollably. I felt so helpless. Yet the Lord kept my sorrow from destroying my ministry; each time He'd pull me back together and help me go on. Now I realize that the Lord accomplished some wonderful victories through me, despite those days of grief. He used me to accomplish real triumphs in His name, and I give Him all the praise for it.

When I called the home of Dick Crittenden to relay the news of his death, his son Craig answered the phone. Dick had asked me to pray for Craig a number of times. As I told the young man about his father's death, his voice choked with tears. In that moment, Craig gave his heart to the Lord Jesus.

I preached the funerals for three of the men—Ron Bayer, who was buried at South Bend, and a double funeral for John and David Harris, buried at Muncie. I didn't preach a message of sweet sentimentality; that would have dishonored the memory of such valiant soldiers of the Cross. No, those funerals were evangelistic services. I preached the gospel and was thrilled to see many people saved.

A good example is what happened at the funeral of John and David Harris. David was the youngest passenger on the plane, only thirteen years old. David wrote and sang beautiful Christian songs, accompanying himself on his guitar. God had used him in a wonderful way at our telethons. At the funeral service, I concluded by asking who would like to give their lives to Jesus Christ. David's classmates from school were sitting together in the audience; they all raised their hands to ask for salvation.

I was so stunned by the accident that I nearly forgot the telethon still going on at WHMB, our station in Indianapolis. But as soon as news of the crash was broadcast, people began phoning in pledges in memory of these five men who had given their lives in the cause of Christian broadcasting. We later used the money to erect a 300-seat memorial chapel at Indianapolis, dedicated in March of 1981. People come here for Bible seminars and evangelistic services, and there is an auditorium where we can tape broadcasts for our network of TV stations.

These and other miracles that have emerged from the tragedy confirm once again the truth of Romans 8:28: "We know that in everything God works for good with those who love him, who are called according to his purpose" (RSV).

LOOKING BACK AT THE TRAGEDY

Christian friends around the world sent telegrams and letters to console us. Billy Graham told me he was praying for me and the men's families "in this great time of trial." Oral Roberts said, "I know how to feel with you, Lester. I lost my oldest daughter and her husband, who meant so much to me, in a plane accident." The messages of consolation and support became a real source of strength in those days just after the accident.

Since that time, I have spent many hours alone with the Lord, trying to discern what He would have me learn from this tragic incident. I have not told the others about this, because all of us have carried a deep sorrow in our hearts, but several times I have envisioned the impact of the airplane. I feel as if God transported my spirit to that time and place as a firsthand witness to what happened, in order to clear up my doubts about the event.

In those times I can see the plane slam into the earth, tumbling end over end, metal shards and human bodies flying everywhere. Then I see all five men in the air about thirty to fifty feet above the plane. They are walking together, looking down at the wreck, and amazement is on their faces.

I hear Dick Crittenden say in his characteristic manner, "Boy, what a mess!"

I see John looking down at the battered plane, shaking his head, and saying, "That's unbelievable!"

They walk around for a few minutes, surveying the damage with idle curiosity, and then they shrug it off as "just one of those things." There's no look of pain, no expression of anxiety on their faces, and soon they are gone.

I well can imagine the reception these men received when they arrived in heaven the morning of the crash! Fresh from the revival campaign, they must have walked through the gates of the celestial city to tell what had happened. "We just replenished the kingdom of God with newborn souls," they must have said. "We encouraged the saints to keep on working till we meet here forever. We had a thrilling time with the Great Commission!"

I miss these partners in ministry, but I know God had finished with them here. He had a greater plan in mind. I am learning to accept that plan. I feel certain that there will be a great harvest for God out of this tragedy. God saved the world by giving His Son to die; tragedy was the price of our salvation. These five men died knowing that Christ died for them, and I believe untold thousands of people will acknowledge the precious love of Christ because of this accident. It's already happening.

LEARNING TO COPE WITH GRIEF

When I first learned of these men's deaths, I wasn't sure I could endure the sorrow. That turn of events was the most stunning blow I had ever received; I was crushed by the loss. But God taught me how to deal with the grief. I learned that grief is a *process*. Grief may last many days or even years. It can be a process of growth or a process of decay. It can change your life for the better or it can destroy you, depending on what you do with your grief.

Grief is sorrow, regret, or depression about anything that may have happened to you. As we'll see in Chapter 5, death isn't the only thing that causes grief. Disappointment or failure can cause it, as can self-pity. You may be shackled by grief at this very moment and not know it.

Ask yourself these simple questions:

• Do my thoughts dwell on what's *wrong* with life, instead of what's good and wholesome and right? (In other words, do I gripe and complain all the time?)
• Do I often have the "moody blues" for some unknown reason? Do I like to sit and brood by myself?
• Am I sarcastic? Do I like to "put down" other people? Do I like to hurt other people?
• Do I feel like a failure? Does it seem as though I never measure up to what I expect of myself—or to what other people expect of me?

If you're a Christian, here are some questions especially for you:

• Have I lost the "joy of my savation"? Am I not as happy as I was when I first was saved?
• Do I hesitate to tell other people about the Lord? Do I feel awkward about my testimony? Have I become a "silent saint"?

Friend, if you answer yes to any of these questions, then something's eating at you. That "something" is grief. Maybe grief is there because you keep thinking about a job promotion you didn't get, a lover who broke your heart, or a financial blunder you made. Whatever the reason, you're grieving about the past, and that grief is destroying you day by day.

18

Because of grief, we live in a nation of dope addicts. I'm not talking about junkies lying on the floors of tenement houses; I mean thousands of decent-looking, "respectable" people hooked on pep pills, sleeping pills, and other drugs because they can't bear life as it really is. They drown their troubles in a shot of whiskey or a cold martini. Or they switch on the TV and turn it up full blast, hoping that the noise will occupy their minds until they can get back to the office or to the assembly line. They can't stand to think about themselves. They can't handle their past. They're afraid to think about their future. Does that describe you?

If you're a Christian with symptoms of grief, you probably feel that way because you became lax about reading God's Word. First Peter 2:2 says, "As newborn babes, desire the sincere milk of the word, that ye may grow thereby;" yet I've seen dozens of new Christians who think they can live without "milk." They read the Bible now and then, only when they feel like it. So they don't grow, and they don't expect the problems they're bound to face as Christians. When those problems come, they whine, "Why me, Lord?" Grief eats them up, because they aren't prepared to deal with it. Does that describe you?

If it does, you must conquer grief before it conquers you!

THE DANGERS OF GRIEF

Grief is not just a passing mood. It can twist your life, even destroy your life, if you let it. For example, King David sometimes let grief get the best of him. His own soldiers criticized his decisions; his cabinet officers talked about him behind his back. I'm sure he sat up many nights with insomnia, thinking about what his friends were saying about him. "I was a reproach among all mine enemies," he said, "but especially among my neighbours, and a fear to mine acquaintance: they that did see me without fled from me" (Ps. 31:11; see also vv. 13,18).

Any leader should know that he is going to make mistakes and that he's going to be criticized; I have yet to see someone make a bold decision that everyone agrees with one hundred percent. Criticism is a fact of life. But when a leader delays the important decisions of today because he's trying to rethink what he should have done yesterday, he's destroying himself. That's the ugly side of grief, and in this sense the Bible says grief is "unprofitable for you" (Heb. 13:17) and "the sorrow of the world worketh death" (2 Cor. 7:10). Grief can be a killer.

Our generation is heavy-laden with grief; the mighty suffer grief, as do the humble. Grief reaches into the royal castles of Europe and America's Oval Office, as well as into hovels and tenements. I have visited over one hundred different countries, and I have seen grief in every one of them. My television talk show, "Today with Lester Sumrall," brings mail from all over the nation describing the most intimate problems of my viewers—and many of them are problems of grief. I know firsthand what grief is doing to our society. That's why I have prepared this series of studies.

HOW THIS BOOK CAN HELP

You see, God has a remedy for grief. His Word tells us what grief is and how to deal with it. In the following pages, we'll take a candid look at what the Bible says about this crippling problem.

This book isn't exclusively for Christians. In fact, if you're *not* a Christian, you have far more to grieve about than a Christian does! You're living in God's world but not on God's terms; you're like a freeloader who tries to sneak past the landlord to live in an apartment house rent-free. You're bound to feel out of place, moody, and depressed if you're not a Christian. You need to read this book very carefully; it can change your entire life.

If you are a Christian this book is just as important, because Christians have grief, too. But God gives Christians special help in times of grief. He can conquer grief.

In December 1961, Dr. S. I. McMillen and his wife received a letter from their daughter Linda, who was a missionary in Rhodesia. She had been hospitalized for several weeks and a spinal tap revealed that she had a deadly tropical form of meningitis. Dr. McMillen writes:

> The news from our only child, nine thousand miles away . . . brought keen sorrow to my wife and me. Never before could we fully appreciate and sympathize with those who had lost their children. Our grief might well have overwhelmed us if it had not been for the comfort and solace of God's Holy Spirit and the Bible. We wondered how people without Christ were able to stand up under great sorrow.[2]

Linda, her husband, and their two small children flew back to the United States, and Linda was admitted to a hospital in Philadelphia. The doctors took several spinal taps, but the dreaded fungus had disappeared. Instead they found pus in the spinal fluid, which indicated that the body was fighting an infection. Linda had a high fever and vomiting, but gradually even those symptoms disappeared. The Lord healed her.

That brush with death drew the entire family closer to the Lord. As Dr. McMillen said later, "Faith can see farther through a tear than through a telescope."[3]

The loss of a loved one—even the threat of a loss—can open our eyes to God's love. Grief can teach us to depend on Him, rather than depending only on our marriage partners, our children, or even ourselves. God does not cause tragedy, but He can bring victory out of tragedy, if we let Him.

NOTES

1. Don W. Hillis, ed., *For More Than a Diamond* (Chicago: Moody Press, 1966), p. 140.
2. S. I. McMillen, *None of These Diseases* (Old Tappan, N.J.: Spire Books, 1963), p. 104.
3. Ibid., p. 105.

2

THE PROBLEM OF GRIEF

Today's world is drowning in grief. Wherever I go on my evangelistic tours, I find people bowed down with the burden of grief.

They slide down the gutter of grief into the pit of despair, where they're ready to give up on life. I don't know how many widows have come to my study sobbing over the death of their husbands, saying, "I don't have anything to live for now." That's despair. I've counseled some of the wealthiest businessmen of our city, and I've heard them say, "Life doesn't mean anything to me anymore. It's a bore." They've hit despair. That's the problem with grief—Satan can use it to make you despair, to make you give up on life.

But despair is not the inevitable result of grief. The Bible tells us that our Savior was "a man of sorrows, and acquainted with grief" (Is. 53:3). He had to be acquainted with grief, or He could not lift us up out of the quagmire of sorrow that is the common lot of us human beings. Yet Jesus did not let grief destroy Him; He did not let His grief turn to despair.

GRIEF AND SIN

How does a person fall into despair? The process always begins with *hidden sin*.

Sin—man's rebellion against God—is what brought grief to this world in the first place. When Adam and Eve decided to disobey God's orders and eat the forbidden fruit, they sinned against Him. When they realized what they had done, they tried to hide themselves from God; I imagine they ducked down behind some bushes and hoped that He wouldn't notice them. But He did. And when God asked why they were hiding, Adam said, ". . . I was afraid . . ." (Gen. 3:10).

If Adam had been faithful to God, he'd not have been afraid. He could have stood before God with a clean conscience. But sin changed all that; sin made Adam a cowering, fearful wretch. And when God passed sentence on Adam for what he'd done, He said, ". . . Cursed is the ground for thy sake; in *sorrow* shalt thou eat of it all the days of thy life" (Gen. 3:17, italics mine). To Eve, God said, ". . . I will greatly multiply thy *sorrow* . . . in *sorrow* thou shalt bring forth children . . ." (Gen. 3:16, italics mine).

Adam and Eve were a "sorry" pair! Even before they suffered the penalty of physical death, they suffered the penalty of sorrow. They grieved over what they had done. They regretted their sin. They lived with that sorrow, grief, and regret for the rest of their lives.

So grief did not begin in heaven. God did not create grief. It is one of the consequences of *sin*.

Some people who experience the tragedy of losing a loved one in a car accident or a plane crash will say, "God must be punishing me because I've not been true to Him. That's why so-and-so died." God does not punish us for our sins in that manner; God does not take fiendish delight in wrecking people's lives. He doesn't go around looking for accidents or tragedies to inflict. These things happen because we live in a world of sin, a world where people suffer and die. The whole human race must live with the consequences of sin. Suffering, death, and grief were not a part of God's plan for us—but we wound up with them because of what happened in Eden. Adam's and Eve's disobedience was the original cause of grief.

However, in many cases, the immediate cause of grief might be sin. People do suffer feelings of sorrow, regret, or anguish because of sin they have commited, although they do not always see that the action was sin.

The Bible gives many examples of people who sinned in ignorance; God still held them accountable for what they did.

Noah cursed the descendants of his son Ham because the young man told his brothers how Noah lay drunk and naked in his tent (see Gen. 9:20–27). Though Ham should not have disgraced his father, there was no written law against what Ham did until the time of Moses (see Deut. 27:16). Ham sinned in ignorance of the law, but he was punished.

When King David brought the ark of the covenant back to Jerusalem, it was carried on an ox cart driven by men named Uzza and Ahio. God's law said that only the Levites could touch the ark (see Num. 4:15). Apparently, these two men were not Levites, but lowly ox drivers. Yet when the oxen stumbled and the ark started to fall off the cart, Uzza reached out to steady it (see 1 Chr. 13:9,10). God struck him dead. Uzza acted instinctively and perhaps without knowledge of the law, but he sinned nevertheless. And so he had to suffer the consequences.

The apostle Paul told King Agrippa how he had sinned in ignorance by persecuting the Christians. Paul had been a zealous Jew who thought he was doing God a great service by tormenting those supposed heretics (see Acts 26:9–12). In fact, he was on his way to Damascus to seek and destroy more Christians when Jesus Himself appeared to him and converted him. Paul wrote to the Corinthians that he was ". . . not meet to be called an apostle, because I persecuted the church of God. But by the grace of God I am what I am . . ." (1 Cor. 15:9,10). Paul sinned in ignorance; yet God forgave his sin.

Old Testament law required a person to offer special sacrifices when he committed a sin unknowingly (see Lev. 4:1ff;

5:4ff.; Num. 15:24ff.). And in the New Testament, Jesus said, "He that knew not, and did commit things worthy of stripes, shall be beaten with few stripes . . ." (Luke 12:48).

Even as He died on the cross, Jesus said of His tormentors, "Father, forgive them; for they know not what they do" (Luke 23:34). They may not have known what they were doing, but they sinned nevertheless. They needed God's mercy. Today many people sin against God in ignorance, simply because they don't know God's standards, but God still holds them accountable.

On the other hand, a person may realize his sin and not be sorry for the sin—just sorry that he has been discovered! Let me share an experience from my boyhood to illustrate this. I stole something from a friend of mine and felt pretty cocky because I had gotten away with it. I felt so sure of myself that I was able to go to bed that night and pray, "Lord, I hope You don't hold this against me." I wasn't sorry for what I had done.

Then my mother found out about it. I knew she would spank me (and she did). From the moment she discovered my sin, I felt sorry—not because I'd sinned but because she had found out about it. I was not grieved because I had done wrong. I was grieved because I knew I'd get a good, sound licking from my mother.

Millions of people live like that. As long as they sin and get by with it, they feel pretty cocky. They think, "Boy, I really pulled the wool over his eyes!" Or, "Man, my wife will never know I'm running around behind her back!" But when someone uncovers their sin, they feel sorry. They're sorry they got caught!

The Bible calls this "hidden sin" or "secret sin." The Psalmist said, ". . . Cleanse thou me from secret faults" (Ps. 19:12); "Thou hast set our iniquities before thee, our secret sins in the light of thy countenance" (Ps. 90:8). Solomon declared, ". . . God shall bring every work into judgment, with every secret thing, whether it be good, or whether it be evil" (Eccl. 12:14).

"Secret sins" are just as serious as the notorious kind. Secret sins lay a heavy burden of guilt—not to mention a burden of fear—upon the heart, and that burden will wear you down.

Arsenic can poison you slowly. Newspapers carry stories of people who die suddenly, of no apparent cause, whose autopsies reveal they were ingesting this deadly chemical for many years in their food or water. Arsenic destroys them by degrees, and so it is with secret sins. You may think you're getting away with your sin, but it is taking its toll on you. Grief over sin is seeping into your life, and one day that grief will turn to despair. Life will lose its luster for you, and you'll want to give it all up.

Francis Schaeffer says, "The basic problem of the human race is sin and guilt—a real moral guilt, not just guilt feelings, and a real moral sin, because we have sinned against a God who is there and a God who is holy."[1]

SALVATION OR SORROW?

Modern man flees to the psychiatrist's couch for relief from his despair. Maybe you haven't actually gone to a psychiatrist; perhaps you've tried to find the answer in self-help books or courses in "positive thinking." These methods can be extremely helpful, when seen in the proper perspective. They can help—but the basic problem that needs to be dealt with is sin.

I have been a minister for over fifty years. I have served some of the great churches in Asia, South America, and the United States. I have talked with the street people of Manila, the mountain villagers of Tibet, and the truck drivers of Chicago. Among every class and nationality, I have found people who just didn't care about life anymore. They existed in despair. And in every case, I found their life had become that way because they were carrying hidden sins.

A desperate person doesn't always look desperate. In fact, a desperate person may paste a big smile on his face and say, "I feel fine today." But that's a lie. Deep inside, sin and guilt are eating him alive. Maybe that's where you are today. You tell everyone you're feeling fine. But you got out of bed with a headache. You yelled at the kids before they could get off to school. Lunch gave you indigestion. Your feet and back hurt, like they always do. (No wonder—sin is a heavy load to carry!) You plod along through life this way, thinking everyone else feels like you do. Then one day you slump on the edge of your bed, stare at the wall with bloodshot eyes, and say, "What's the use of living?" That's despair. And it proceeds from sin.

As I mentioned in the first chapter, sin can give you a "godly sorrow" that leads to salvation (2 Cor. 7:10), or it can bring despair. Dr. W. A. Criswell notes:

> No one comes to Christ and salvation without sorrow for his sins. But sorrow in isolation produces only death. . . . When a man recognizes his sinfulness and helplessness in sorrow for his failure, he has a mind to seek God by faith in Christ. The inevitable result of this genuine repentance is a renewed interest in spiritual matters (2 Cor. 7:11).[2]

That renewed interest causes a person to call upon the Lord. Godly sorrow moves a sinner to repent of his sins, confess that only Jesus can save him from them, and believe that Jesus will be true to His word (see 1 John 1:9).

But if you try to hide your sin, you'll find no forgiveness from God. You will get no relief from your guilt. You will feel the threat of death hanging over you, like a mighty sword ready to slash your neck. This is what 2 Corinthians 7:10 means by the phrase, the "sorrow of the world." Ungodly grief brings a host of destructive emotions, often the most visible signs of what is really happening inside you. Let us briefly examine some of these accompaniments to ungodly grief.

Bitterness

Scripture says, "Follow peace with all men, and holiness, without which no man shall see the Lord: Looking diligently lest any man fail of the grace of God; lest any root of bitterness springing up trouble you, and thereby many be defiled" (Heb. 12:14,15). Bitterness is a jealous, resentful attitude toward another person. It springs from envy and hate. You may be bitter toward your mate, your boss, your parents, or someone else because you secretly wish you were like them. Perhaps someone has taken advantage of you; you're bitter because you wish you'd taken advantage first. No matter what the source of your bitterness, you can be sure it wouldn't have started if you had tried to "follow peace with all men." If you had really shown the "grace of God" toward that person, if you had given him only God's love regardless of what he gave you, you would not be bitter. You would still love that person. You would still have a sweet spirit.

Instead, you look back at what has happened and grieve, because you wish you'd taken the upper hand. You would like to live the moment over again, so you could "get back" at the other person. That's bitterness.

Hate

That great preacher of the last century, Henry Drummond, said an ill temper "is the intermittent fever which bespeaks unintermittent disease within; the occasional bubble escaping to the surface which betrays some rottenness underneath. . . ."[3] That's a perfect description of hate!

The hateful person flares up suddenly to criticize the people around him. Unlike the bitter person, who holds a grudge that everyone can see, the hateful person holds a deep-seated grudge that occasionally explodes into fits of vile rage. Like a volcano, he builds up enormous pressure, then "blows his top" at the least provocation. Hate is a "rottenness underneath" his otherwise peaceful exterior.

You may think you are a mature, well-controlled person, but if you fly into fits of rage now and then, you're not as mature as you think. Just because your hatred has a "safety valve," don't fool yourself into thinking it's gone away. The fits of temper show otherwise—and such displays are never "safe."

Anger and Sadness

Anger and sadness are more closely related than you might suppose. When a person gets intensely angry, you can let him "cool off" and he will become intensely sad. Why? Because he knows he has done wrong.

While bitterness and hate focus on one person or a certain group of people, anger is more generalized. Any number of things might provoke your anger—a child's toy underfoot, a careless driver on the freeway, a customer who can't make up his mind. Once your anger is loosed, you are irritable with everybody. You mutter things like, "Doesn't *anybody* know how to drive these days?" Or, "Why do I get *all* the stupid clients?" Or, "*Nobody* cares about quality anymore."

Is it any wonder you feel sad? You think you're all alone in the world. You believe no one else is as neat or as punctual or as conscientious as you are. You feel as though you live on a lonely island in a sea of incompetence.

They say that time heals all wounds. Not so for the angry person. Time just deepens the wound and rubs salt into it as one tirade follows another. The angry person lives a life of cynicism and despair.

Dejection

Anger often leads to dejection. When you feel someone has rebuffed your friendship or declined your overtures of kindness, you feel rejected, dejected, downcast. You think nobody loves you anymore.

If I had a dollar for every time I've been rejected by someone, I'd be the wealthiest man in the world. People who watch our worship services on television or attend one of our evangelistic crusades may be impressed by the hundreds who come forward to accept Christ or to be delivered from illness. But many, many more people refuse to come. From the pulpit I see the faces of people who long to be saved from their sins; some of them have tears streaming down their cheeks. But when I invite them to come to the altar and pray, they hold back. They don't come. They reject me and the message of my Lord. Can you imagine how I would feel if I took all of that rejection to heart?

Charles L. Allen tells the story of a university president who had a young professor with a habit of making brash statements to the press. The teacher spoke out on controversial issues. His ideas upset some of the merchants in town, who withdrew their support from the school. One day the president invited the professor to a chapel service in which the president extolled the great diplomacy of Jesus, stressing that Jesus was a tactful man who gently won over His critics to His point of view. After the service, the young professor shook the president's hand and thanked him for the message. "But I have one question," he said. "If Jesus was so beautifully tactful and diplomatic, how did He manage to get Himself crucified?"[4]

No one can be accepted and liked all the time—not even

Jesus! We must learn to live with criticism and snubs. We must not let them fester in our souls and grieve us.

After suffering multiple rejections, the apostle Paul wrote to his friends at Corinth, "We are troubled on every side, yet not distressed; we are perplexed, but not in despair; persecuted, but not forsaken; cast down, but not destroyed; . . . For we which live are alway delivered unto death for Jesus' sake, that the life also of Jesus might be made manifest in our mortal flesh" (2 Cor. 4:8,9,11). Paul saw defeat in its proper perspective. He did not become dejected. He knew that even the setbacks could glorify the Lord.

Timidity

When I speak of timidity I don't mean the awkward shyness of a thirteen-year-old; nearly everyone goes through a shy stage in the process of growing up. I mean the timidity caused by guilt. For example, I know several middle-aged men who can't stand to mingle in crowds because they are self-conscious of their sin. Ask them to speak before a group, and they'll stammer and sweat because they are afraid they might reveal what they have done.

Preying on unconfessed sin, Satan can plant seeds of doubt in the Christian's mind to make even the child of God bashful. Often Christians have told me, "I can't witness to people. I'm just too shy. I wouldn't know what to say." That's the Devil speaking. What he's really whispering is, "You're not good enough to speak up for Christ." How do I know? Because it contradicts the very words of Jesus, who said, "When they bring you into the synagogues, and unto magistrates, and powers, take ye no thought how or what thing ye shall answer, or what ye shall say: For the Holy Ghost shall teach you in the same hour what ye ought to say" (Luke 12:11,12).

Lately we have heard a great deal about people who are shy

by temperament or "by nature." But I don't find any exceptions like that in the New Testament. I don't find Jesus saying, "Go ye into all the world and preach the gospel to every creature—unless you are shy" (see Mark 16:15). There are no exceptions. He just says, "Go . . . preach . . . teach . . . baptize . . . For the Holy Ghost shall teach you in the same hour what ye ought to say."

Fear

Fear is one of the most crippling emotions that comes with grief. I have seen people worry themselves to death, so frightened of the future that they dread going to work each morning. They double-bolt every door at night and tremble when they hear a noise outside. They live in a shell of cowardice, smothered in fear.

In the early days of the Cold War, when the United States and Russia edged to the brink of a nuclear hell, Chaplain Peter Marshall offered this prayer in the U.S. Senate:

> Our Father, give us the faith to believe that it is possible for us to live victoriously even in the midst of . . . crisis. Help us to see that there is something better than patient endurance or keeping a stiff upper lip, and that whistling in the dark is not really bravery. . . .[5]

If we trust our own strength and wisdom—our weapons, our computers, our wealth, our dead-bolt locks—we have good reason to be afraid. All these things can fail. None of them can give us full security.

But if we trust Jesus Christ, the Creator and Savior of this world, we find that He "casteth out fear" (1 John 4:18). Jesus said, ". . . If God so clothe the grass of the field, which to day is, and to morrow is cast into the oven, shall he not much more clothe you, O ye of little faith? Therefore take no thought, saying, What shall we eat? or, What shall we drink? or, Wherewithal shall we be clothed? . . . for your heavenly Father knoweth that ye have need of all these things. But seek ye first the kingdom of God, and his righteousness; and all these things shall be added unto you" (Matt. 6:30–33).

Again Jesus said, "Let not your heart be troubled: ye believe in God, believe also in me" (John 14:1).

Why should you be afraid? Why should you dread what your enemies might do to you? ". . . Greater is he that is in you, than he that is in the world" (1 John 4:4). If you have surrendered your life to Jesus Christ, then the Lord of all the universe is taking care of you.

GOD'S ANSWER TO GRIEF

The Bible says that God created us to be joyful, not sad. "For the kingdom of God is not meat and drink; but righteousness, and peace, and joy in the Holy Ghost" (Rom. 14:17). Even when we fall on hard times and God seems to have forsaken us, His Word promises that He will bring us joy again. "Sing unto the LORD, O ye saints of his," the Bible says, "and give thanks at the remembrance of his holiness. For his anger endureth but a moment; in his favour is life: weeping may endure for a night but joy cometh in the morning" (Ps. 30:4,5).

Recently I wrote a book entitled *Ecstasy: Finding Joy in Living* (Nashville: Thomas Nelson, 1980). The theme of that entire book was God's plan to bless us with joy and happiness, although Satan has deceived people into thinking otherwise. In that book I said something that needs to be repeated here:

> *You can be happy every day of your life.* Your exterior situation does not have to dictate your interior attitude, unless

you let it. What shows whether or not you are a happy person is not what happens to you, but how you react to what happens.

Similar problems descend upon different people; some let the problems get them down, while others are able to rise above the problems and grow stronger because of them. It all depends on what's inside. A person who has Christ reigning in his heart can have joy permanently. . . .[6]

Every week I encounter people who have been tricked by Satan into thinking that they should be melancholy or sad. "I'm just fretful by nature," they say. "I'm easily moved to tears." Or, "Guess I'm just moody by nature."

If you're fretful, weepy, moody, or short-tempered "by nature," it's by your *carnal* nature. Those emotions are not a sign of God's "new" nature within you (see 2 Cor. 5:17). As long as we are on earth we will be plagued by these feelings and moods, but all of the destructive emotions described in the preceding pages are aberrations of what God intended for you.

Jesus Christ came to set us free from the world's troubles. Now I don't mean that if you become a Christian you'll be protected from all trouble; you'll still have things like illness, disappointment, and overdue bills to pay. But if you give your life to Jesus, He will enable you to rise above these troubles. He will give you a sense of victory, even in the midst of trouble. He will loose the binding shackles of despair and let your heart sing, "It is truly *wonderful* what the Lord has done!" (see Is. 25:1). Remember that precious promise from Jesus Himself: "If the Son therefore shall make you free, ye shall be free indeed" (John 8:36).

So many people live in bondage to grief and the destructive emotions that grief can bring! In the Philippines a Chinese businessman came to see me one day. He arrived in a beautiful Cadillac with a uniformed chauffeur. When he entered the gate of our garden, he was holding his hands stiffly in front of him.

They looked leprous, puffy and swollen. I walked down into the garden to greet him, but he refused to shake my hand, saying, "You might give me a disease by shaking hands."

The businessman then explained that he had touched nothing with his hands for ten years, for fear that he would contract a disease and die. His chauffeur confirmed this. Even when he signed a business contract, he immediately would lay down the pen, wash his hands, and disinfect them. (I can imagine how this made his business associates feel!) His life was now overwhelmed with this fear, the manifestation of the grief and despair deep in his heart.

I asked the man if he would like to be free from his tormenting fear and grief. He said he would. I laid hands upon him and rebuked the spirit of fear in his heart. Immediately the Spirit of the Lord came upon him and the joy of the Lord entered his life. The man stretched out his hand to me and I gave him a firm handclasp. By this time a large crowd of curious passersby had gathered in the yard. Noticing them, the businessman stooped down and gleefully rubbed his hands in the dirt. He then turned, opened the gate himself, and opened the door to his limousine for the first time in ten years. He was free from his unbearable fear.[7]

THREE STEPS TO FREEDOM

So how can you find freedom from the destructiveness of grief? How can you let go of the past? How can you stop worrying and start living? Let me outline three steps that you can follow:

First, *realize how destructive grief can be*. Remember, grief is more than just sorrow over someone who has died. People commonly give the word that narrow meaning, but grief is much more. One college dictionary defines grief as "Deep sorrow or mental distress caused by loss, remorse, affliction, etc."[8] So you see, grief is much broader than bereavement; grief is any form of "deep sorrow or mental distress." The emotions of loneliness, regret, defeat, torment, anger—any of these may be signs of grief.

When you find these emotions churning inside you, name the problem for what it is. Say, "Lord, I'm grieving. Show me what's causing it." The first step to ridding yourself of the problem is naming it for what it is. Don't try to slough it off with excuses. Face the fact. Find out what is bothering you, and realize what grief can do to you. Grief won't go away by itself; you must tackle it head-on and take control of it.

Dr. Robert H. Schuller, pastor of the Garden Grove Community Church, tells of a beautiful girl named Barbara who visited his office. Barbara had cerebral palsy and all four of her limbs were paralyzed. Doctors had told her she would be handicapped the rest of her life, and one day would be mentally retarded. But Barbara decided to make the most of what she still had. She worked with a doctor to design special braces and metal supports so that, by using certain muscles, she could walk again. "With God all things are possible," she said. "I decided that nothing was going to stop me!"[9]

That's the attitude you must have toward your grief if you intend to conquer it. Realize its threat to you. Realize what it's doing to you. Name it for what it is. Then you'll be ready to deal with it.

Second, *rebuke the grief in your life*. You must renounce the spirit of grief, just as I rebuked it in that Chinese businessman. Command it to leave you. Renounce its claim over you. If the grief has such a powerful grip that you can't renounce it, seek the help of someone who can.

Recently a lady from Ohio drove to our Christian Center Church in South Bend and came to the altar for prayer. She said Satan kept telling her she wasn't saved; that was all she could think of. I prayed with her and renounced this spirit of doubt, then taught her how to rebuke Satan if he ever tried to make her doubt again.

If you're not a Christian, you're probably not used to rebuking Satan. You're used to obeying him. *Only God can give you the power to renounce Satan.* And the only way to receive God's power is to receive Jesus as Lord and Savior. No matter how forceful and persuasive you are with other people, you are no match for the "prince of the power of the air" (Eph. 2:2). The Bible tells about seven young men who tried to rebuke an evil spirit in the name of Jesus Christ, even though they weren't Christians. The evil spirit cried out from its victim and said, "Jesus I know, and Paul I know; but who are ye?" (Acts 19:15). Then the demon-possessed man leaped on them and ripped their clothes off.

These destructive spirits are nothing to trifle with. For your own sake, claim the God who does have the power to defeat them.

Third, *claim the blessing God has for you.* I don't have enough space here to list all of the gracious promises of God's Word. But He offers a special blessing for you, depending upon your need and the ministry He has given you. Here is just a sample of the blessings He offers:

Are you sorrowing over the death of someone? God says, "They that sow in tears shall reap in joy. He that goeth forth and weepeth, bearing precious seed, shall doubtless come again with rejoicing . . ." (Ps. 126:5,6). "And God shall wipe away all tears from their eyes; and there shall be no more death, neither sorrow, nor crying, neither shall there be any more pain: for the former things are passed away" (Rev. 21:4).

Are you holding a grudge against someone? God says, ". . . Walk worthy of the Lord . . . Strengthened with all might, according to his glorious power, unto all patience and longsuffering with joyfulness" (Col. 1:10,11). "Grudge not one against another, brethren, lest ye be condemned: behold, the judge standeth before the door. Take, my brethren, the prophets . . . for an example of suffering affliction, and of patience" (James 5:9,10).

Are you fearful about your future? God says, ". . . Take no thought, saying, What shall we eat? or, What shall we drink? or, Wherewithal shall we be clothed? . . . for your heavenly Father knoweth that ye have need of all these things. But seek ye first the kingdom of God, and his righteousness; and all these things shall be added unto you. Take therefore no thought for the morrow . . ." (Matt. 6:31–34).

I could go on, but these are enough Scriptures to show you the pattern. Every time you let go of grief or some grief-related emotion, God offers you a blessing. Let go of sorrow and He gives you joy; let go of a grudge and He gives you patience; let go of fear and He gives you provision. It's like the rhythm of a trapeze artist, who must let go of one rung so he can fly through the air to another. If he doesn't let go of the first rung, he can't catch the next. If you don't let go of your grief, you can't receive God's blessing.

My friend and co-worker in the Lord, Jerry Falwell, has endured many hardships in building the work of Thomas Road Baptist Church and the "Old-Time Gospel Hour" television program. He has faced financial trouble, criticism, and all the other problems that plague an evangelist who preaches the straight gospel truth. Yet Jerry says:

> I look back and can recount some dark days and bitter experiences. They were all God's teaching plan for Jerry Falwell. You can recount those horrible and gruesome times when you thought you would die. All that time God was teaching you.[10]

If you can see the promises of God behind the cloud of grief and despair, you will find your way out of the grief. Name it for what it is, rebuke Satan's power, and claim God's promises in place of it.

NOTES

1. Francis A. Schaeffer, *True Spirituality* (Wheaton, Ill.: Tyndale House Publishers, 1971), p. 94.
2. W. A. Criswell, ed., *The Criswell Study Bible* (Nashville: Thomas Nelson Publishers, 1979), p. 1370 n.
3. William R. Webb, ed., *The Greatest Thing in the World* (Kansas City, Mo.: Hallmark Editions, 1967), p. 18.
4. Charles L. Allen, *Perfect Peace* (Carmel, N.Y.: Guideposts, 1979), pp. 28,29.
5. Catherine Marshall, *Mister Jones, Meet the Master* (Old Tappan, N.J.: Spire Books, 1966), p. 161.
6. Lester Sumrall, *Ecstasy: Finding Joy in Living* (Nashville: Thomas Nelson Publishers, 1980), p. 149.
7. Lester Sumrall, "Break the Hex and Return the Curse," *World Harvest*, July-August 1978, p. 10.
8. *Funk and Wagnalls Standard College Dictionary* (New York: Harcourt, Brace and World, Inc., 1963), p. 590.
9. Robert H. Schuller, *It's Possible!* (Old Tappan, N.J.: Spire Books, 1978), p. 20.
10. Gerald Strober and Ruth Tomczak, *Jerry Falwell: Aflame for God* (Nashville: Thomas Nelson Publishers, 1979), p. 59.

3

FATAL
FASCINATIONS

Some snakes can hypnotize their prey. The snake's unblinking, beady eyes and gently swaying body hold the attention of a bird while the snake creeps closer, then strikes. The victim is caught.

The same sort of thing is happening in our world on a much larger and more devastating scale, affecting human lives. Millions are drawn into grief—devoured by grief—because they are fascinated by it. They can think only about the awful things that might happen to them.

One day President Gerald Ford talked with a group of us from the television media in his White House office. With a frown he said, "Gentlemen, five hundred good things could happen in this city, and you wouldn't get a line of it in your newspapers or on television. But let one bad thing happen and the media will blow it to the sky."

That's the way our world operates today. The news broadcasts on radio and TV are filled with voices of gloom that chant the litany of war, famine, suffering, and economic woe. The mass media have become harbingers of grief, focusing on what is evil and corrupt in this world. In the words of the late William Randolph Hearst, "It sells papers."

Things such as auto crashes and terrorist raids make bold headlines and cause a sensation. Our society has grown to expect this type of fare from the news media. Even daily conversations reflect this morbid preoccupation. No longer do people make conversation with, "How do you like this weather?" They begin with something like, "Did you see that traffic jam on Main Street? Terrible!" Or, "Isn't this inflation eating us alive?" Or, "Did you hear about that robbery at the grocery store last night?"

People begin and end their day with worry. They live on dismay. They are hooked on tragedy.

I even have heard some preachers do this. Every time they enter the pulpit, they begin a tirade about the gloom and doom that's swirling around us, saying that we're about to see the end of the world. Now I would agree that we're about to see the end of the world; the Bible makes that plain enough. But that makes it all the more urgent for us to preach the *gospel*. We need to show people how to find victory for every day. Who cares about counting down to Armageddon if you're not prepared for it? I'm afraid that a lot of the end time preaching that we hear today doesn't come from a desire to spread the gospel; it comes from a desire to cause a sensation and draw big crowds. I don't want to make a sensation. I want to help you find joy and gladness in your life. Jesus said, ". . . If I be lifted up . . . [I] will draw all men unto me" (John 12:32). He's proven that over and over again in my ministry. When I lift up the saving name of Jesus, the crowds come. I don't need shock tactics to draw a crowd.

OTHER FASCINATIONS

The fascination with tragedy is the most obvious way in which grief has hypnotized this world. But grief has other fascinations, too, some of them very plain, others subtle—and thus more deadly.

First, there is the fascination of *survival*. I see this in the nations of the Third World that I visit each year. People are struggling just to stay alive. From the time they get up in the morning until they lie down to sleep at night, the uppermost thought in their minds is, "Where will I get something to eat?"

or, "Where can I find clothes to keep me warm?" In a situation like that, it's hard to think of joy or victory. These people have no idea that their lives could be any better.

Eric Hoffer wrote a book on political revolution called *The True Believer,* in which he describes this problem. Hoffer said:

Where people toil from sunrise to sunset for a bare living, they nurse not grievances and dream no dreams. One of the reasons for the unrebelliousness of the masses in China is the inordinate effort required there to scrape together the means of the scantiest subsistence.[1]

If you have ever visited Hong Kong, as I have, and talked with the refugees from Red China, you know what Mr. Hoffer is saying. The Communist government of China stays in power not because it is a good government or because it is the best choice the Chinese people have. It stays in power because the people are so busy trying to stay alive, they have no time to think about change.

The same is true of several million people in the United States. We like to think there are no hungry or homeless people in this country, but there are. In my home state of Louisiana, I know of many people who live in tumbledown shacks and rummage their food from garbage cans. Ask any mortician, and he will tell you that people who have no place to live still die on the streets of exposure. They simply lie down in the gutter and die.

These people are fascinated by survival. It is useless to talk with them about being saved or finding joy in life. They will look at you as if you came from another planet; you're talking about something utterly alien to them. You must begin by helping them get the food, clothing, and shelter they need. You must break the deadly spell that grief holds over them. Then they will be ready for the gospel.

43

There is the fascination of *failure* or *defeat*. When the auto companies laid off thousands of workers in recent years, the unemployed often slipped into grief. They sat at home day after day, not even willing to go to collect their unemployment checks. They felt defeated; they felt destroyed. Life held no more meaning for them. Bus workers from our church in South Bend have found scores of people in this condition. It is a tragic thing to see.

You may fall into the same sort of thing in a more subtle way. You may let the daily frustrations of life crowd out any sense of joy; you may let things "bug" you so much that you live with defeat all the time.

Linda Dillow, a minister's wife, confronted a problem that would defeat many other women: When her family moved into an old house near Cornell University (where her husband had a campus ministry), they had no water. The well had gone dry. They had to carry in water for cooking and drinking and had to bathe at a neighbor's house.

Linda easily could have felt defeated. She could have grumbled about the water problem. She could have felt bitter toward God for calling them to such a place. But she didn't. She claimed the promise of Romans 8:28 and trusted God to work it out for the good.

That's exactly what God did, too. During her trips to take baths and wash dirty diapers, Linda talked with her neighbor about starting a neighborhood Bible study. On her trips to the grocery store, she heard many people say, "Aren't you the folks with the water trouble?" and she had a chance to tell how God was helping her family through it. Then her husband prayed about finding a site for a new well; the landlord drilled where the Lord said to drill, and they found the best well in the neighborhood. The experience challenged the landlord to have more faith in the Lord. Linda writes:

There are difficult circumstances in the life of every person, in every marriage. We each have a choice; when the hard times come we can put up our fists and fight with anger and resentment, or we can give the situation to God and trust He will cause good to come out of even a bad situation. The first choice breeds discontent and frustration. The second breeds the fruit of the Spirit: love, joy, peace, patience, kindness, goodness, gentleness, and self-control.[2]

Yet another subtle fascination of grief is the fascination of *bad habits*. Some of us secretly love our bad habits; that's all we can talk about. We say we'll give up smoking or overeating or drinking. But we don't do it because, deep inside, we cherish those habits. They are familiar and comfortable to us. We'd rather suffer the consequences than risk giving them up.

A friend of mine who ministers to college students spent one whole night sharing the gospel with a homosexual. This "gay" student knew he was living in sin. He heard the gospel and seemed on the verge of making a decision for the Lord, but he kept holding back. He said he didn't think he could stop being a homosexual.

My friend said, "You know, a lot of boys go through a stage where they're attracted to other boys instead of to girls. They like to 'pal around' with other guys. But the Lord has made our bodies in a marvelous way; our bodies change when we reach our teen-age years. God gives us a sex drive that attracts us to the opposite sex. It's all a part of growing up.

"Let me put it to you straight," my friend said. "I think you don't want to stop being homosexual because you're afraid of growing up."

The homosexual looked surprised.

"When I was a boy, I had a big teddy bear that I liked to sleep with," he continued. "That teddy bear was warm and cuddly. It made me feel secure. Even after I was a teen-ager, when I felt frightened or lonely I'd sometimes go back to the closet and get that teddy bear because it made me feel so good. But when I came to college, I had to leave that teddy bear behind. I had to be a man. I had to find my security in Jesus Christ instead of in some stuffed toy. In 1 Corinthians 13:11, Paul says, "When I was a child, I spake as a child, I understood as a child, I thought as a child: but when I became a man, I put away childish things.'

"Bob," he said, "homosexuality is your teddy bear. You're holding onto that because it is comfortable and secure. You're afraid to let go of what is familiar. If you'll turn your life over to Jesus, He'll help you put that teddy bear away, and you'll never need to get it out again."

That young man gave his life to Christ and made the commitment to put his homosexual ways behind him. And Christ helped him become the man he was made to be.

NO STRANGER TO GRIEF

Joseph Fort Newton wrote, "God did not make us to be eaten up by anxiety, but to walk erect, free, unafraid in a world where there is work to do, truth to seek, love to give and win."[3] That's what Jesus came to do. He came to set you free from fear. He came to lift the load of worry. He came to wipe out the debtsheet of despair. My friend, Jesus came to set you free. And that's all I care to do in my ministry.

I feel I must set the record straight about my own experience with grief. Many people see me on television week after week, proclaiming a message of hope and deliverance, and they say, "That's easy for him to believe—he never had to face what I'm up against." Maybe not. But you should know what I have faced.

I know how it feels to lose all of my closest friends in an instant. That plane crash in Indianapolis gave me more sorrow than I'd care to see anyone carry. Yet the Lord brought me through it.

I know what it is to watch a child die. My youngest brother, Archie, died at the age of eighteen months. We loved him dearly because he was the last child of the family, and there was nothing we could do to save him. Yet the Lord brought me through it.

I know what it is to see working partners go bankrupt. I have wept and prayed with precious friends who lost everything they owned, then struggled to help them get on their feet again. Yet the Lord brought me through it.

I know what it is to hold the hand of a young, able-minded Christian dying of cancer. I have felt the last pulse of life ebb away, then walked out into the waiting room to break the news to a stunned family. Yet the Lord brought me through it.

Friend, I don't preach the good news of Jesus Christ because I have led a sheltered life. I don't promise you deliverance from grief because I just don't know any better. I have lived with tragedy; I know what it is. And I know that Jesus Christ can turn it into victory.

I have found tragedy and heartache in some of the most unlikely places. How well I recall visiting the home of the postmaster in a little Eskimo village eighty miles north of the Arctic Circle. They have no radio or TV up there, so for entertainment after dinner we sat around the table and browsed through the Sears and Roebuck catalog. After a while I excused myself and went to bed. Then an argument broke out around the kitchen table.

"That's too expensive!" I heard the husband yell. "You don't need any fancy dress like that!"

"Oh, yeah?" she shouted. "That's 'cause American woman good enough for you. Eskimo woman too good. You don't know class when you see it!"

I laughed so hard I could scarcely go to sleep. Here they

were, hundreds of miles from the nearest high society dinner party, and they were arguing over a cocktail gown. Why, it was so cold the only thing anyone could wear was a parka! Yet they were quarreling, and she went to bed crying. It was high comedy and grim heartache.

For five months I lived among the Indians in the jungles of Brazil. Each evening I sat around the campfire and listened to the Indians talk, with my interpreter whispering in my ear. One night I saw the natives laughing among themselves, sneering at me from a distance. I asked what was wrong.

"You can't ask us to be Christians," they said, in a tone of ridicule.

"Oh? Why's that?"

"The Christian soldiers—they kill us," the Indians said. "We don't want to be Christian."

"Would you like to be a follower of Jesus?"

"Oh, Jesus—that sounds good. We would be Jesus persons, but not Christians. Christians are killers."

Sophisticated city-dwellers may think the "noble savage" has no worries; but his sorrow is just as real and painful as any other person's. His deprivation is as great. His fear is just as binding.

I was once invited to eat lunch at Hampton Court Palace in London, because a member of the royal family had a deep sorrow I was asked to heal. I have found great sadness in a beautiful castle high in the Swiss Alps. I have counseled a man in despair in the executive suite of a powerful bank. I have found that tragedy is no respecter of persons; it plays no favorites. I have learned that it can destroy any person on the face of this earth.

But God has not called me to exploit people's grief. He has given me a ministry of love and caring. When I go to a foreign country, I feel immediately drawn to the poverty-stricken and hopeless masses. My spirit reaches out to them. I feel compelled to walk the streets and alleys of those nations, seeking the ones who most desperately need help. I want to point them beyond their tragedy to Jesus Christ.

Jean Paul Richter once said, "Courage consists not in blindly overlooking danger, but in seeing it, and conquering it."[4]

Faith in God is not whistling in the dark. It's not turning your back on tragedy and saying, "Ignore it. Maybe it'll go away." No, faith in God confronts life head-on. It accepts all of life, the bitter and the sweet, and praises God for it. That's the kind of faith God has given me. It's the kind of faith I want to share with you.

LET GO OF IT!

At the beginning of this chapter, I described how a bird can be hypnotized by the eyes of a snake. In the same way, I said, the world is taken with grief. Its gaze is fixed on trouble. Does that describe you?

Then God can break the spell.

God can snap you out of it.

God can help you conquer grief.

Susan Gift Porter contracted polio at the age of four. She was confined to her bed for many months and thought she might never walk again. Her mind was flooded with so many other fears: What if her parents died? Who would take care of her then? Where would she live?

As it turned out, Susan was able to walk again, but those fears still haunted her. They paralyzed her spirit as the polio had paralyzed her legs. Susan was so full of fear that she couldn't even spend the night at her grandmother's; she feared her parents would die while she was away. When she reached her teens, Susan wanted to be a Christian ventriloquist. She wanted to tour the country and speak before youth meetings. But she was afraid to learn how—afraid to leave home to go to school.

"How will I ever get over these fears?" she asked her mother one evening. "I'll never be a whole person. I'll have to depend on you and Dad forever!"

"Just a minute," her mother said. "I want to show you something I read last night."

She returned to her Bible and pointed to 2 Timothy 1:7: "For God hath not given us the spirit of fear; but of power, and of love, and of a sound mind."

"You know, Susan," her mother said, "either that verse is true or it isn't. I believe it's true. In fact, I believe you can stake your life on it. You need to do that. You need to surrender your fear to God."

"Mom, I've tried. I just don't know how!"

Susan's mother thought about it for a long moment. Then she said, "You haven't surrendered your fear to God because you don't trust Him enough. It's like taking a letter to the mailbox and opening the slot, but hanging on to one corner of the envelope. Then you wonder why an answer never comes."

Her mother kissed her good night and left the room. Susan pondered what her mother had said.

"God, I'm really in a terrible mess," she prayed. "Help me let go of my fears. I really want to be a different person. But I can do it only if You take the fear out of my life."

From that night on, God began to work a miracle. Susan went to the public library and started reading about ventriloquism. She attended Cedarville College and earned a degree in speech and drama. She began touring the country, practicing the ministry God had called her to. She was able to let go of fear and let God take control of her life.[5]

You can do what Susan did. You can let go of the thing that grieves you. You can snap out of the deadly spell that grief holds over you by claiming the promise of His power.

Archbishop Fenelon of Cambrais, France, was the spiritual

advisor to a number of Christians in the court of King Louis XIV. Fenelon wrote several letters of encouragement and advice to them. In one letter, Fenelon stressed the need to let go of doubts and cares:

> If we have strength and faith enough to trust ourselves completely into the hands of God, and follow Him wherever He leads us, there will be no need of stretching and straining to reach perfection. But since we are so weak in faith, and always stopping along the way to ask questions, our journey is lengthened and we get behind in spiritual development. So you see how important it is for you to abandon yourself as completely as possible to God, and continue to do so until your last breath. . . .[6]

The Christians of every age have rediscovered this timeless truth: We must be willing to let go of our grief and let God conquer it.

CHRIST THE BURDEN-BEARER

Jesus said, "Come unto me, all ye that labour and are heavy laden, and I will give you rest" (Matt. 11:28). A lot of people are carrying a load that Jesus has already offered to carry for them. When He went to the cross to die, He picked up your sorrows and problems. He's carrying them for you. You shouldn't try to keep carrying them yourself.

A certain Methodist bishop was so troubled by the problems of his district that he stayed up late one night, gazing into the fireplace. He wearily dropped one log after another onto the fire and sighed, "Oh, my! What am I going to do?"

At last the clock struck twelve. The bishop heard a voice behind him.

"Go to bed now," the voice said. "Get some sleep. I'll stay up the rest of the night and worry for you."

The bishop looked up and smiled. "I'm sorry, Lord," he said. "I should have known better. I should have laid my burdens at your feet to begin with."

You need to bring your sorrows, your hurts, your sadnesses, your griefs, and lay them all down at the Master's feet. Just say, "Lord, You're the Burden-bearer. You promised to carry these things for me. So I'm laying them down before You and I'm going to leave them with You."

Some of us bring our problems to the Lord, but then we pick them up again. We're so fond of nursing our grief that we wouldn't know what to do without it. We like to tell other people about our problems so they will respond with reassurance and pity; we wouldn't have that if we gave up our grief. So we try to carry it ourselves. We tip our hats to Jesus and say, "I'm glad to know you're my Savior," and then we try to save ourselves. Our grief just gets bigger and bigger.

One minister I know had a terrible fear of flying on planes. He avoided them whenever he could. When an emergency call required him to catch a plane to the West Coast, he knew he would have to face this fear head-on.

On the plane he settled himself in the seat, nauseated with fear. He thought he'd have to use the airsick bag before they got off the ground! But then he entered into a prayer conversation with the Lord, and it went something like this:

"Lord, You know I'll never make it to California in this condition."

"That's right," the Lord said.

"Well, can't You help me get over this awful fear I have?"

"Of course I can," the Lord said, "if you'll give it to me."

"How can I do that?"

"Open your briefcase."

That seemed like a strange order, but the minister did so.

"Now, take out an envelope and sheet of paper," the Lord

said. "Write FEAR on the sheet of paper. Fold it up and put it in the envelope. Seal the envelope."

"What now?"

"Hold the envelope in front of you," the Lord said. "Let all of your fears flow into that envelope."

The minister felt a little silly sitting there with that envelope in his hands. But the Lord sometimes asks His people to do strange things, so the man obeyed. He let all of his fears flow into the envelope. He could feel the tension leave his head. He felt his stomach relax.

"When all of your fear is in the envelope," the Lord said, "let it go. Just let the envelope fall to the floor."

The minister let it go.

The plane taxied down the runway and took off. For the first time in his life, the minister enjoyed flying. He looked through the window at the tiny houses below, and a broad smile crept across his face.

Before long the plane hit some turbulence. The aircraft rose and fell like a crazy elevator. The minister felt his fear coming back.

"What do I do, Lord?"

"Pick up the envelope."

The minister did as the Lord told him, and again he had to let all of his fear flow into the envelope. In a few moments he let it drop to the floor again. He had to repeat the procedure several times, but by the time he arrived, his fear of flying was gone forever. Now he loves to fly.

An old gospel song says, "Take your burden to the Lord and leave it there." That's exactly what you must do if you want to break the grip that grief holds on your life. Surrendering your problems to Him may take some practice, but you must learn to let Christ the Burden-bearer do the work He came to do.

When you insist on keeping your burdens, you deny God's

Word. You deny the Lord Himself. You're saying, "I don't trust You, Lord." That's a sin. Unconfessed and unsurrendered grief is just as wrong as thievery, lying, or any other form of spiritual rebellion. So let's name it for what it is.

Oscar H. Hirt has written a precious little book on the Twenty-third Psalm called *The Shepherd and His Sheep.* Here's what he says about the Lord's promise to give us rest, when we give our burdens to Him:

> Now the Shepherd uses His authority to give provision *and* rest to the sheep in His green pastures and He gives this rest by satisfying them completely. A sheep will go on walking long after it is weary, but the moment it is satisfied, it will lie down. Are you satisfied, with the Lord Jesus? with what God has provided for you? Then lie down and rest![7]

Satisfaction is really the crux of the surrender problem, isn't it? If you won't surrender your grief to the Lord, it must be because you're not satisfied with what He can do. If you *are* satisfied, you'll let Him do His work. You'll let Him bear your burdens. You'll let Him save you from your sins. Fritz Ridenour says, "There is no magic in faith. Faith is simply our response to the salvation Christ obtained for us."[8] In a nutshell, that's what I'm saying. If you believe Christ really saves you from sin and grief, you'll have no problem surrendering it to Him.

You can have problems and yet have peace, if you give those problems to the Lord. When I purchased the television station in South Bend, I put my signature to a one-million-dollar indebtedness. That was a problem! Yet I knew the Lord wanted that station for our ministry, so paying off the debt was the Lord's problem, not mine. I had peace. And the Lord took care of that problem in short order: in just a little over a year, the station was paid off.

Jesus Christ has purchased our peace. The Bible says He *is* our peace (see Eph. 2:14). Why should we try to buy again something that has already been purchased for us—especially when we can never afford to buy it ourselves? Nothing in this world can buy peace for us. The law courts can't; drugs can't; liquor can't; illicit sex can't; and money surely can't. Nothing we possess can buy peace of mind and rest for our souls. But Jesus has already bought it for us, and He freely offers it to us. We can trade in our burdens for peace. I'd say that's quite a bargain!

CONFESSION BREAKS THE SPELL

If you're caught in the trance of grief, I urge you to give that grief to Jesus. No matter what caused your problem, Jesus can bring good out of it. You can break the spell by naming grief for what it is. Confess you've sinned against God by holding this burden back from Him. Confess that the grief itself is a sin.

Charles Swindoll tells how Beethoven pushed himself to keep on composing great symphonies even after he went deaf. Loss of hearing is a handicap that quickly defeats a musician if he lets it. But Beethoven would not give in to defeat. He kept pounding the piano harder and harder, determined to *feel* the notes if he could not hear them. One of his neighbors said that on an especially frustrating day, the genius banged on the keyboard with his fist and shouted, "I shall take life by the throat!"

Dr. Swindoll adds that every one of us must take our problems "by the throat." If we try to pretend we have no problem it can destroy us.[9]

I challenge you to face your grief today. Take a sheet of paper and pencil and write down the name of what's bothering you.

Maybe it's *lust* . . . Write it down.

Maybe it's *hate* . . . Write it down.

Maybe it's *fear* . . . Write it down.

Whatever the name of your grief, write it down. Just use one or two words. Sin is really a very simple thing to describe. Don't use long phrases to put frilly excuses around your grief; just write down what it is that keeps hounding you, soaking up your energy, and crippling your witness for God. When you can name your grief, you've taken the first step to surrendering your grief.

When he rededicated his life to the Lord, Keith Miller (author of *A Taste of New Wine*) wrestled with this problem of naming sin. He learned that he had to be specific. When he prayed for forgiveness, he had to label sin as *sin*, or he could not find peace with the Lord. In his own words, Keith started to "keep short accounts with God":

> . . . Instead of saying "Lord, today I exaggerated a little on my expense account, but you know everyone else does," I was able to say, "Lord, I *cheated* on my expense account today. Help me not to be a dirty thief." Or instead of saying, "Lord, I couldn't help noticing that secretary down the hall . . . it was such a windy day . . . but Lord you know that boys will be boys," I began to be able to level with God and to say openly to him, "Lord, I thought of sleeping with that girl. . . ."[10]

My, how Satan hates honesty! He knows that when we name our sin and confess it to the Lord, confession breaks his spell. It snaps us out of the deadly trance of grief. We may feel helpless under grief, but we're not. We still have the power to confess our grief to God and let Him take the burden of it.

Today you face a crucial choice that will determine the rest of your life and your destiny in the hereafter. The choice is simply this: *Will you let grief be your master, or will you let Jesus Christ be your Master?*

In this chapter we have seen that grief can be a cruel master indeed. It can choke all the joy from your life. It can afflict you with sleepless nights, ulcers, frayed nerves, and a befuddled mind. It demands your constant attention, consumes every idle moment of your day, and may even intrude on your dreams. Is this the kind of master you want?

If you are fascinated by grief, you won't be able to set yourself free. Every day that you mull over your grief is another link in a mighty chain that holds you fast to the rockpile of despair. Your fascination becomes a "fasten-ation." Every day grief forges another link in the chain that you can't snap by yourself. But Jesus can!

Remember the stirring promise of Charles Wesley's hymn, "O for a Thousand Tongues":

> *Jesus, the name that charms our fears,*
> *That bids our sorrows cease;*
> *'Tis music in the sinner's ears,*
> *'Tis life, and health, and peace.*
>
> *He breaks the power of canceled sin,*
> *He sets the pris'ner free;*
> *His blood can make the foulest clean,*
> *His blood availed for me.*

That's the gospel truth, my friend. Jesus' precious blood, shed on the cross of Calvary, has purchased peace for you. His sacrifice has bought freedom for you. Instead of entertaining your grief, confess it, and leave it with the Lord. He alone can set you free.

NOTES

1. Eric Hoffer, *The True Believer* (New York: Perennial Library, 1966), p. 33.

2. Linda Dillow, *Creative Counterpart* (Nashville: Thomas Nelson Publishers, 1977), p. 161.
3. Ralph L. Woods, ed., *Courage Is . . .* (New York: Essandess Special Editions, 1968), p. 41.
4. Beatrice Brown, ed., *Lines of Inspiration* (New York: Westport Corporation, 1974), p. 31.
5. Susan Gift Porter, "The Promise that Overcomes Fear," *Guideposts,* January 1981, pp. 26–29.
6. Fenelon, *Let Go!* (Springdale, Pa.: Whitaker House, 1973), p. 53.
7. Oscar H. Hirt, *The Shepherd and His Sheep* (Upper Darby, Pa.: The Bible Club Movement, Inc., 1972), p. 10.
8. Fritz Ridenour, *How to Be a Christian Without Being Religious* (Glendale, Calif.: Gospel Light Publications, 1967), p. 28.
9. Charles Swindoll, *Hand Me Another Brick* (Nashville: Thomas Nelson Publishers, 1978), pp. 190–205.
10. Keith Miller, *A Taste of New Wine* (Waco, Tex.: Word Books, 1965), p. 59.

4

WEEP NO MORE

Grief over death is one of the most prevalent and destructive forms of grief. Millions of people are mourning for loved ones who have died. Some will grieve themselves into an early grave, so this kind of grief is a very serious matter. The word *grief* comes from the Latin *gravis,* meaning "heavy." Any kind of grief brings a heaviness of heart, but this is especially true when a person grieves over death. The grief of death can make one feel listless and "mopey" and, if allowed to go on, can bring physical illness and death.

A group of researchers at the Institute of Community Science in London made a study of 4,486 widowers in that city. They found that, in the first six months following the death of their spouse, forty percent more of these men died than would have been the average. Alvin Toffler writes that this study "strongly suggested that the shock of widowhood weakens resistance to illness and tends to accelerate aging."[1] Researchers have found similar results in the United States.

Many people simply cannot accept death. They don't know how to respond to it when it comes, so the grief of death hits them hard.

On "Today with Lester Sumrall," I recently interviewed a young man named Randy Stilly. Randy is a male nurse at one of the hospitals in South Bend. I think his comments shed some light on this problem of the grief over death:

Sumrall: As a male nurse, I'm sure that you see a lot of grief over death.

Stilly: Yes, even in born-again Christians. It seems that many people cannot grasp that God loves them, that He is their loving Father. I try to demonstrate to the people I meet the kind of love God shows for us.

Sumrall: Throughout the day, you visit one hospital bed after another. Do you find that just as many men have grief as do women?

Stilly: Oh sure, just as many.

Sumrall: You meet poor people and wealthy people. Is there any difference in the way grief affects them?

Stilly: Money doesn't make a bit of difference.

Sumrall: Do you find that people are more willing to talk about their grief when they are in the hospital? Are they more willing to receive help with their grief?

Stilly: Yes, they are. Their defenses are not up. They know they are in trouble and need help. I've found that a few kind words, spoken in God's love, can carry a power and anointing to set these people free.

Sumrall: Randy, you are quite an unusual person. With the scientific instruments of your profession, you can see what is physically wrong with a person. But with your spirit you can hear and see much deeper than that. You see the spiritual needs of the people and are willing to show them that Christ is the answer.

Stilly: That's right—He's the only answer to their grief. He is our Father. He loves us and cares for us. When my patients realize that and can free their hearts from grief, they begin to heal. God can heal their bodies when the emotions are straightened out.

This young man knows firsthand what grief can do to people. It can weigh down the emotions and bend the logical processes of thinking. It can tense the nerves and drain the physical reserves of the body. Grief can kill. This is especially true of bereavement—grief over death.

WHY GRIEVE OVER DEATH?

In counseling with people grief-stricken about the death of some loved one, I've found that they were vulnerable to grief because of their own attitudes toward death.

Some have deep grief because *they fear their own death*. They are upset to see their mate or some close relative die because the event seems to bring the dreaded time of their own reckoning that much nearer. These people suspect that death will bring changes—but they are not sure what those changes will be. They fear a person is snuffed out at the moment of death, as a candle flame is snuffed by a sudden draft. They don't want to be destroyed. This, by the way, is why people take such pains to be sure they are remembered. The psychologist Theodore Lidz says:

> . . . Individuals seek many ways "to cheat drowsy death" and somehow perpetuate themselves—that is, one's name, ideas, ways of doing things, one's "flesh and blood"—from oblivion. The desire for descendants in whom one lives, who will carry the name or keep alive even a spark of memory of one's existence . . . The structures they build, be they indestructible pyramids or more useful bridges, dams, or buildings . . . Through joining their lives to a more abiding organization, a church, philanthropic movement, or library or orchestra . . . How individuals strive for it provides a key to understanding many aspects of their behavior.[2]

Indeed it does! I'm sure you have friends who are obsessed with "making a name" for themselves. They seem to be in a race with the clock, trying to erect some eternal monument to themselves before death comes. They think that after death, no part of them will remain except the memories.

The world's mourning customs reflect this. I lived in China for several years and had opportunity to observe traditional Chinese funerals. Chinese families feel that they cannot grieve enough for their dead, so they hire professional mourners to march in the funeral parade. I say "parade" because that's exactly what the funerals are—loud, showy processions through the streets of town. Mourners are paid to wail and weep uncontrollably; you'd think these mourners had lost the dearest person in the world! Their task is to impress the *memory* of the dead person upon the community.[3]

I also noticed how Chinese families observe the Festival of the Unforgotten Dead. During this biannual festival, Chinese families bring offerings of food, flowers, paper money, and paper images of servants to the tombs of their ancestors. Since the Chinese believe their dead ancestors are still there (just invisible), the food and gifts are supposed to be used by the dead. But of course, they say, these things can only be used spiritually; so the worshipers burn the money, flowers, and images, and eat the food themselves!

Like others around the world, these people do not want to admit that death changes anything. They prefer to think that death is only a passing over from the visible to the invisible world. Better that, than the idea that death is the end of life, and the dead will be soon forgotten.

The Japanese have a similar festival in July each year, called the Festival of the Dead. Japanese families place food and drink offerings on the altars in their homes, because they believe their dead ancestors are coming back to visit them. At night they light lanterns or candles to guide the unseen visitors. Tourists think this is a quaint custom, and so the custom has also been called "the Festival of the Lanterns." The basic idea is the same as the

Chinese: the ritual is a way to pretend that death changes nothing.

Our American funeral customs are based on the same pretension. We embalm bodies so they will appear natural. In fact, when the deceased has suffered a ravaging illness, the embalmer may make the body look *better* than natural! We visit the bereaved family in a funeral home and view the body, which has been made up into a suitable "life image." The coffin is lined with soft velvet and lace, with thick pillows for "comfort." Every aspect of the preparation of the corpse is designed to tell the family and friends that the deceased is merely sleeping. This is unique to the United States. Embalming is unheard of in Europe and other parts of the world. (Even the Irish wake—Europe's closest approximation to a "viewing" of the body—has passed from the scene.) "In order to sell death," one writer says, "it had to be made friendly."[4]

LIFE AFTER DEATH

No matter how we try to deal with it, death still remains a stranger. Death *does* change things.

For the deceased, death changes the place of residence. Instead of living at 1234 Main Street, when you die you will go to live in heaven to worship God forever or to hell to be tormented with Satan forever. The Bible says that you don't float around in limbo from the time you die, waiting for the Day of Judgment. You go immediately to your new residence, and on Judgment Day you are assigned permanent living quarters there!

Remember Jesus' parable of the rich man and Lazarus? He said that when the beggar died he "was carried by the angels into Abraham's bosom" (Luke 16:22), while the rich man went to hell (v. 23). Jesus said to the thief who repented on the cross,

". . . To day shalt thou be with me in paradise" (Luke 23:43). Because this man repented of his sins and confessed Jesus as his Savior, he went straight to heaven that day.

The Westminster Confession, that great statement of Christian faith, gives us a clear word about what happens to people when they die.

Based on the Scripture I have just noted (and many other texts), the confession says:

> The souls of the righteous . . . are received into the highest heavens, where they behold the face of God in light and glory, waiting for the full redemption of their bodies.[5]

On the other hand, the confession says that when ungodly people die, they are immediately "cast into hell, where they remain in torments and utter darkness, reserved to the judgment of the great day."[6] That is, the wicked must be tormented until the Day of Judgment; then they are permanently consigned to the "lake of fire" to be tormented forever (see Rev. 20:10,12–14).

I stress this point because some people believe the dead are wandering around on this earth, waiting for the Judgment Day. They believe they should try to communicate with the dead or, like the Chinese and Japanese, pretend that the dead are still living with them. These ideas are contrived by human superstition and custom. The Bible tells us what really happens. We need to trust it instead of our own ideas.

For those who are left behind, there are many changes in the areas of companionship, family ties, financial needs, living quarters, and so on. Death's impact on the life of a marriage partner especially is devastating. The Bible says that when two people marry, they become "one flesh" (Gen. 2:24). So when one partner dies, the effect is radical and painful as if the body has been torn apart.

A widow may sit by her window day after day, as if un-
plugged from life. Activities that once gave joy and meaning to
her now seem empty and senseless. She withdraws from friends
and pays little attention to her health or appearance. She has lost
someone very important to her, and she needs to get her bear-
ings on life again without that person. Widowed men often act
the same way.

Death does bring a change to everyone involved; there's no
use denying it. But there's no need to fear death either.

Some people fear death because they think it brings suffering. They may have seen pictures of dead soldiers with their
faces contorted in pain or heard stories about the final agony of
accident victims in the hospital. They imagine that all people
suffer intense pain in the last throes of death. Their fancy runs
wild because they have not seen people die. Professor Keith
Watkins writes:

> . . . Death is less real to people now than it once was. We see so
> little of it, especially during childhood and the early adult years.
> In the city instead of on the farm, we no longer watch animals
> portray before our eyes the cycle of birth, maturation, old age,
> and death. . . .[7]

Not seeing death becomes a very real problem. I wish more
families would spend time around the deathbed of a beloved
grandparent or other relative, so they would know that death
usually is not a painful thing. I have kept the vigil with many
families, and I know that death is the end of a physical suffering. Usually it is a welcome thing. For the Christian, it is the
start of untarnished joy forever in heaven.

These are a couple of reasons people fear their own death—
reasons why they grieve so much over the death of someone
they love. People who grieve for these reasons need to understand what death really is.

Some people have a deep grief because *they depended on the dead person for their own life*. All of us have seen pitiful examples of this: The husband who does not know how to prepare his own food, wash his clothes, or do other basic household chores because his wife did them for the past fifty years; the wife who does not know how to drive the car, budget her income, or balance her checkbook because her husband always did that. When their spouse dies, such people suddenly must make tremendous changes, which they may not be able to handle.

You'll recall the British study of widowers, which I mentioned at the start of this chapter. After asking why so many widowers died soon after their wives did, Alvin Toffler said, "The answer may lie . . . in the very high impact that loss of a spouse carries, forcing the survivor to make a multitude of major life changes within a short period after the death takes place."[8]

I recall the case of a retired couple who had been married more than forty years. When the husband retired from his factory job, they bought a retirement home near the Gulf of Mexico so they could fish together. Their new life was a dream come true. Then the wife died of a heart attack. The husband was stunned by the loss. Their retirement dream vanished into thin air. His wife was dead, his children had scattered, and now he had to learn to live on his own. A few months later he entered the hospital for routine surgery and died on the operating table; his doctor said he'd lost his will to live.

This type of thing is common. When a person is cut off from his source of support and life and finds no way to sustain himself, he gives up his will to live. His spirit gives up and soon his body follows suit. It simply stops functioning.

In 1967, Dr. W. Dwei Rees of Wales studied the families of 371 people who had died in his district. His findings were even more astonishing than the London study. He reported that

66

widows and widowers died at *ten times* the normal rate during the first year of their bereavement; other close relatives died at *five times* the normal rate during that year. When Dr. Rees published his findings in the *British Medical Journal,* he called this phenomenon the "broken heart syndrome."[9]

Some bereaved people commit suicide for this reason. They can't bear the thought of starting a new life without their mate, their parents, or someone else who was their life support. They would rather kill themselves than try to adjust.

Suicide has become a leading cause of death among teenagers and is gaining in notoriety as a killer of adults. According to recent data from the U.S. Department of Health and Human Services, the suicide rate is highest among people over the age of seventy.[10] People in this age bracket feel the impact of widowhood more than others. Undoubtedly, many suicides committed by elderly people stem from their grief over losing a husband or wife. Helen Hosier notes:

. . . The forgotten and lonely elderly, feeling useless, un-needed, and a burden to their family or society, choose suicide—yes, death seems better than four walls, no companionship, and the inevitable suffering that accompanies ill health in old age.[11]

Again I must emphasize: *Grief is a killer.* If allowed to rule your life, grief can destroy you through illness and emotional disorder. It can even compel you to take your own life. How vitally important, then, that you learn to recognize grief in your life. How crucial that you learn to conquer grief!

GRIEF AND DEPRESSION

The grief of death often leads to depression. Since death does bring abrupt changes to a family, there are good reasons to be emotionally upset. When a loved one dies, we cry. We cry for ourselves. We cry because we know that life won't be the same without the companionship of that person. That kind of grief is healthy. It helps us realize that we must rearrange our lives. We must make allowances for the gap the dead person will leave in our lives. But if we sorrow over a prolonged period of time, our grief may turn into depression. This is dangerous.

A *depressed* person withdraws from other people. He gives up hope for moving ahead with life. He will not listen to reason or encouragement. The depressed person makes himself an island separated from the rest of humanity, because he fears getting hurt again. He doesn't want to get involved in a close, loving relationship because he knows that death will someday enter that relationship, too. He can't handle death. He tries to retreat from it.

Only recently have doctors realized that depression is an illness, like schizophrenia or other mental disorders. Depression interrupts the biological processes of the body. Backaches, headaches, dizziness, upset stomach, and insomnia are some of the chronic symptoms of a depressed person. A doctor may see a patient with these problems and treat the symptoms, without realizing the cause. After months of tests and medication fail to bring a cure, he may question the patient more closely and uncover grief over someone's death. Such a state calls for a different kind of treatment. Drugs and therapy may ease the *symptoms* of depression, but only a change of mind can lift the *cause* of depression. Frank Ayd, research director of Taylor Manor Hospital in Ellicott City, Maryland, interviewed five hundred victims of depression and learned that they had gone to over fifteen hundred specialists. "They kept asking for more tests," Dr. Ayd says, "because they couldn't believe they didn't have a brain tumor."[12]

The symptoms do seem like those associated with cancer or

some other fatal disease. While there's nothing organically wrong with the person, the mind sends out distress signals that the body obeys. Illness sets in. If the person is physically weak at the outset, sudden death may result.

All of us should be alert to these danger signals in our friends, especially when someone dear to them has just died. They are more apt to feel depressed in their time of sorrow, and if they slip into the valley of depression, someone needs to set them on the road back to a normal life.

A person's depression will also affect his family and friends, spreading like a tidal wave and drowning hope. I have even seen depression stifle the life of a church.

Once I was invited to preach at a Methodist church in the Philippines. The sanctuary had a divided chancel; the pastor gave the Scripture reading from a lectern on one side of the platform, while I preached from a lectern on the other side. The altar stood between us.

Seated along the middle aisle was a beautiful, middle-aged lady who looked extremely sad. Throughout my sermon, she looked extremely depressed. Nothing I said affected her.

After the service, I walked down the aisle and shook hands with the congregation. This lady took my hand and said, "How do you do?"

I said, "You are very sad, aren't you?"

"Yes," she said. "My husband was an elder of this church, and he died recently." (I later learned that he had died nine months before.) "We are all so sad about it . . ." her voice trailed off.

I see now what is wrong with this church, I said to myself. *This body is dying of grief. Lord, help me to be a spiritual surgeon who can cut this cancer out of the church before it destroys them all.*

"You say your husband died several months ago?" I said. "It is too bad he went to hell."

The woman's eyes flashed with anger. "He didn't go to hell!" she shouted. "He went to heaven!"

"I see. So it just *looks* like he went to hell. If your husband went to heaven, why don't you smile about it?"

Her anger rose higher. She tapped her foot in rage.

"Tell me, what color of clothes is your husband wearing in heaven?" I said.

"White!"

"Then why do you still wear your black mourning dress?" I asked.

The woman whirled around to leave. "Where are you going?" I asked. But she hurried on out the door.

I turned around and saw the pastor staring me in the face. "Do you realize what you've done?" he gasped. "Those people are millionaires. They are the best members of my church."

"Yes, but that woman is inflicting a spirit of grief on the congregation," I said. "You cannot preach to them in that condition."

I ate lunch with the pastor that day, but I don't think he enjoyed having me there. I stayed in my room that afternoon preparing for the evening message, because I sensed that he did not want to talk with me.

But God worked a miracle in the heart of that woman. My comment about her clothes made her think. When the time came for the evening service, she appeared at the door in a dazzling white gown, with white stockings, white shoes, and a white silk headpiece. Best of all, she was wearing a beautiful smile.

The cloud of gloom lifted from that congregation. Joy came upon the people, and we had a marvelous service that night—all because one woman accepted what the Lord Jesus Christ tells us about death.

A CHRISTIAN'S VIEW OF DEATH

Granted, death will bring dramatic changes to your life. Adjusting to those changes will be hard for you, and you will feel sorrow for awhile. But one day you must pick up the pieces of your life and go on. A humanistic pep talk won't help you do that, but the truth of eternal life and the resurrection can.

I have looked at the majestic Rocky Mountains and thought how marvelously those granite giants endured so many centuries of earthquake, wind, and rain. But you and I will outlast the Rockies. Those mountains will be burned up when Christ returns (2 Pet. 3:10,12), but we will still be alive. The Bible says that when the world is destroyed, ". . . We shall not all sleep . . ." (1 Cor. 15:51); that is, we won't be snuffed out of existence. ". . . But we shall all be changed. In a moment, in the twinkling of an eye, at the last trump [i.e., trumpet]: for the trumpet shall sound, and the dead shall be raised incorruptible [i.e., never to decay or die], and we shall be changed" (1 Cor. 15:51,52). You and I are destined to get new bodies that cannot die (see Phil. 3:21; 1 John 3:2), and in these new bodies we will stand before God to be judged.

What a wonderful hope this is for bereaved people! When I saw the battered bodies of my friends at that morgue in Noblesville, I was shocked and overwhelmed with grief. But I was greatly comforted by the knowledge that one day they will have new bodies, perfect and everlasting bodies, that can never be injured again. Our earthly bodies will decay. But the heavenly bodies God will give us can never decay, for they are "incorruptible."

Clothed in these new bodies, the dead shall rise to stand before the judgment seat of God. There He will separate the "sheep" from the "goats" (Matt. 25:31–46), the saved from the unsaved. He will punish the unsaved by casting them into the lake of fire, where they will suffer with Satan and his demonic hordes forever. But He will take the saved into heaven to enjoy eternal life with Him. Until that great Judgment Day, the dead wait in heaven or hell, depending on whether they accepted Jesus Christ as their Savior in this life. If you have any doubt about where your dead friend or relative is right now, just look at the Word of God.

I have conducted many a sad funeral for people who had not accepted the Lord. When their relatives looked to me for comfort I could only say, "There's nothing more we can do. This person is in God's hands now. God will reward him according to His Word." That's the heartbreaking truth.

But for the Christian who dies, we should celebrate. Shed no tears for the victor.

As he neared the end of his earthly life, the apostle Paul wrote, "I have fought a good fight, I have finished my course, I have kept the faith: Henceforth there is laid up for me a crown of righteousness, which the Lord, the righteous judge, shall give me at that day: and not to me only, but unto all them also that love his appearing" (2 Tim. 4:7,8). A Christian who stays faithful to the end is like a marathon runner who finishes his race, overcoming all the obstacles and hazards that would have deterred him. Why should you weep and be sad when that happens? You may feel a little sad for yourself because you must wait awhile to see that person again. But shed no tears for the dead in Christ. They are in the winner's circle.

When Dr. Peter Marshall died of a heart attack, his widow Catherine sat on the hospital bed and held the hand of the corpse for nearly an hour. She thought of the wonderful life they had known together. But she also felt the reassuring presence of the Lord, who reminded her that she must go on with life. Finally, she knew she had to leave her husband's body.

As I rose to go, I knew that this was farewell to the earthly part of the man whom I loved; farewell to the touch of his hand, to his warmth, his gaiety, his flashing smile.

"Till death do us part," we had vowed on our wedding day, as we had stood before the flower-banked altar. And that physical tearing apart is very hard for us who are still so human, who are still of the earth. . . .

But . . . my path was lit by celestial light. Around me was all the glory of heaven. It was as if Peter, joyously stepping over that invisible boundary that divides this life from the next, had left the curtain pulled aside, letting heaven through so that we . . . could share a little of his joy and understand better what was happening to him. . . .

I would not give the impression that I did no crying during those days. I did. There were times when I wept copiously. But there was not bitterness in the tears, only emotional release, and between-times God gave me a quiet mind and a steady heart.[13]

Through God's Word, we know that all of our friends and relatives who die in the flesh are still alive in the spirit. If they have surrendered their lives to Christ, they are now with Him and are waiting to welcome us home. I still remember the night I received a cablegram telling of my mother's death. I was preaching in Japan. The cable simply gave the time and day Mother had died, and when I checked my watch I found that she had entered heaven at exactly the time I was in the pulpit expounding the Word. My heart rejoiced. For so many years, Mother prayed that I would become an evangelist, and she was thrilled to see the Lord call me to gospel work when I was still in my teens. I could think of no more fitting place to be when she entered the gates of glory.

Yes, it is natural to cry when a friend or relative dies; but God can wipe away our tears with the truth. He can remind us of the "blessed hope" that waits for all Christians beyond the door of death (Titus 2:13).

LET GO OF GRIEF

The poet James Weldon Johnson left us a funeral sermon that says:

> *Weep not, weep not,*
> *She is not dead:*
> *She's resting in the bosom of Jesus.*
> *Heart-broken husband–weep no more;*
> *Grief-stricken son–weep no more;*
> *Left-lonesome daughter–weep no more;*
> *She's only just gone home.*[14]

Johnson's sermon is the essence of what I've been saying in this chapter. Weep no more for your Christian dead; they've gone home with the Lord. You and I should be preparing to do the same. The glorious destiny of every Christian is to die and join Jesus Christ, to reign with Him in eternity. Such a fate is no cause for tears. Paul wrote, "Therefore we are always confident, knowing that, whilst we are at home in the body, we are absent from the Lord. . . . We are confident, I say, and willing rather to be absent from the body, and to be present with the Lord. Wherefore we labour, that, whether present or absent, we may be accepted of him" (2 Cor. 5:6,8,9).

I have talked with many hospital patients who suffered terminal illness. If any of these people were not Christians, I shared the gospel and talked about what to expect after death. Many, many of these patients accepted the Lord—the only sensible choice when you stand on the brink of eternity.

I have urged those who were Christians to remember their witness. Unsaved people watch a Christian as he approaches the hour of death, to see whether he really believes what he says. Fear and grief have no place in the Christian sufferer at a time like that, for they deny the very gospel itself. Again, Paul said, "I am crucified with Christ: nevertheless I live; yet not I, but Christ liveth in me: and the life which I now live in the flesh I live by the faith of the Son of God, who loved me, and gave himself for me" (Gal. 2:20).

For the sake of your witness, let go of grief. Fix your mind on the victory that will be yours when you go home to Jesus, where your loved ones already are. You will be a "seal" of God's truth to the people who see you; you will prove that His "love is strong as death" (Song 8:6). God will give you "beauty for ashes, the oil of joy for mourning, the garment of praise for the spirit of heaviness; that [you] might be called trees of righteousness, the planting of the LORD, that he might be glorified" (Is. 61:3).

For the sake of yourself, let go of grief. "A merry heart maketh a cheerful countenance: but by sorrow of the heart the spirit is broken" (Prov. 15:13). Your physical health depends on being able to put sorrow behind you and follow after the Lord. Your spiritual life depends upon it.

So weep no more. Your companion in the Lord is not dead. He's only just gone home.

NOTES

1. Alvin Toffler, *Future Shock* (New York: Random House, 1970), p. 286.
2. Theodore Lidz, *The Person,* rev. ed. (New York: Basic Books, Inc., 1976), p. 538.
3. I have not been back to mainland China since the Communist takeover, so I do not know whether such funeral processions are allowed there now. But I believe they are still fairly common in Chinese communities elsewhere.
4. Philippe Aries, *Western Attitudes Toward Death,* trans. by Patricia M. Ranum (Baltimore: Johns Hopkins University Press, 1974), p. 99.
5. Quoted by Louis Berkhof, *Systematic Theology* (Grand Rapids, Mich.: William B. Eerdmans Publishing Company, 1941), p. 679.
6. Ibid., p. 680.
7. Keith Watkins, *Liturgies in a Time When Cities Burn* (Nashville: Abingdon Press, 1969), pp. 109, 110.
8. Alvin Toffler, *Future Shock,* p. 286.

9. David Hendin, *Death as a Fact of Life* (New York: W. W. Norton and Company, Inc., 1973), p. 170.
10. *The World Almanac and Book of Facts* (New York: Newspaper Enterprise Association, Inc., 1980), p. 148.
11. Helen Kooiman Hosier, *Suicide: A Cry for Help* (Irvine, Calif.: Harvest House Publishers, 1978), p. 72.
12. Jane See White, "Depression: 'Curtain of Gloom' an Illness," *Ft. Wayne News-Sentinel*, February 3, 1981, p. 2C.
13. Catherine Marshall, *A Man Called Peter* (Old Tappan, N.J.: Spire Books, 1951), pp. 250, 252, 254.
14. James Weldon Johnson, *God's Trombones* (New York: The Viking Press, 1927), p. 27.

5

GRIEF CAN REDEEM OR DESTROY

Grief is like nitroglycerine. In small amounts properly controlled, it can relieve pain (as nitroglycerine relieves chest pains in a heart victim). In large doses, it can kill. In abundance it can explode, killing the sufferer and innocent bystanders as well. We should realize that grief is volatile. Depending on how we handle it, grief can heal us or blow us to bits.

In the first chapter, I pointed out that the Bible describes two kinds of grief (2 Cor. 7:10). There is a "godly sorrow" that redeems our life from sordidness and sin. There is also "the sorrow of the world," which can kill us. Let's take a closer look at these two kinds of grief.

DESTRUCTIVE GRIEF

"The sorrow of the world" may be caused by many things. For example, we have already seen that destructive grief may arise from *fear of the unknown*. People are afraid of death because they don't know what it will bring. Jesus' disciples cowered behind closed doors after He was crucified (John 20:19), because they thought Jesus was dead forever. They forgot what He had predicted about His resurrection, even when Mary Magdalene told them He had risen. They feared for their lives. When they should have been out in the streets shouting, they met secretly to grieve—all because they feared the unknown.

On one of his radio broadcasts, Dr. Charles Swindoll told about his own fear of the unknown. He was making a long trip by car and stopped at a gas station. When he entered the restroom, he met a stranger.

"You traveling east?" the stranger asked.

"Yes," Dr. Swindoll replied.

"So am I. Why don't we travel together?"

"No, I don't think so."

"Sure!" the stranger said. "We can split the cost of gas."

"No, thanks."

"It won't be any problem at all. I'll sleep most of the time anyway."

"No," Dr. Swindoll said.

"You can use the company," the stranger persisted. "It's better than traveling alone."

"No."

At last the stranger left the restroom. Then Dr. Swindoll came out, got in his car, and drove away. A few miles down the road, he had an uneasy feeling that someone was in the car with him. He noticed a blanket that had been draped over an ironing board in the back seat had slipped partly to one side. He thought, *That guy is a stowaway! When we get to some deserted stretch of road he'll mug me!*

Remembering that he had a crescent wrench under the front seat, Dr. Swindoll pulled off at the first exit to deal with his unwelcome guest. He stopped at the curb, pulled out his wrench, and flung open the back door to confront . . . nothing!

"I'm just glad no one could see me that morning," Dr. Swindoll said. "To think that I had worked myself into such a frenzy over an ironing board!"

Well, people have gotten ulcers over lesser things. They are so afraid of what might happen to them that they let it rule their lives. Grief over the unknown future robs their joy today.

A husband may think his wife is unfaithful, when in fact she is not. He may be short-tempered for no apparent reason, making her life utterly miserable because he suspects she's having an affair with another man.

A parent may think his child is rebellious and impose harsh rules to make him "toe the line." The parent's fear of the unknown alienates him from the child. That fear becomes a self-fulfilling prophecy. The child rebels because he thinks Mom or Dad doesn't love him anymore.

Fear of the unknown is a destructive thing; even Christians can be ravaged by it.

Idol Worship

Destructive grief also can arise from *idol worship,* which I define as any tendency to place trust in a creature of God, rather than in the Creator. Supposedly the first-century Romans were the most intelligent people of their day, but Paul said, "Professing themselves to be wise, they became fools, and changed the glory of the uncorruptible God into an image made like to corruptible man, and to birds, and fourfooted beasts, and creeping things. . . . and worshipped and served the creature more than the Creator, who is blessed forever. Amen" (Rom. 1:22,23,25). We see these same characteristics in the Eastern religious cults that are gaining a foothold in America; pagan idol worship is coming back into style.

More subtle forms of idol worship are also destroying America. Spiritualism, black magic, and astrology are some examples of teachings that encourage people to put their faith in tea leaves, tarot cards, push-pin dolls, and planets, rather than in God.

Idol worship in all its forms will bring a person grief. The idol worshiper feels an emptiness and gloominess that he can't explain, although his heart knows why those feelings are there. He's trusting fallible gods; he's pinning his hopes on things that will not last. "For other foundation can no man lay than that is laid, which is Jesus Christ. Now if any man build upon this foundation gold, silver, precious stones, wood, hay, stubble; every man's work shall be made manifest; for the day [of judgment] shall declare it, because it shall be revealed by fire; and the fire shall try every man's work of what sort it is" (1 Cor. 3: 11–13).

Skepticism

Destructive grief can arise from *skepticism toward the grace of God*. Nineteenth-century evangelists like Dwight L. Moody, R. A. Torrey, and Billy Sunday lashed out against *skeptics* of the gospel. We seem to think that's an old-fashioned term, but the skeptics are still with us. If anything, their number has increased.

The twentieth century has thrust us into a wondrous garden of knowledge, where philosophy and the sciences bloom more profusely than ever before. But with great learning comes great conceit, at least when man's depraved nature has control, so the decision-makers of our age ridicule the Christian faith with disdain. Two prize-winning historians furnished proof of this when they dismissed the role of Christianity with comments like, "It was fear that first made the gods," and, ". . . It is pleasant to be relieved of theological terrors, to enjoy without qualm the pleasures that harm neither others nor ourselves, and to feel the tang of the open air upon our liberated flesh."[1] That is skepticism, doubting that God knows what is best for us.

The skeptic soon discovers there is no life or joy without Jesus Christ. If he refuses to accept the offer of salvation through Christ, he becomes "hardened through the deceitfulness of sin" (Heb. 3:13). A hardened skeptic falls into despair, believing that life is a meaningless lark that ends in nothing.

A Christian physician recently asked a friend, "What do you think happens to a person after he dies?"

"When a person dies," the other doctor said, "he becomes fertilizer for the flowers."[2]

That's the philosophy of skeptics. They have closed their minds to the gospel.

The Channel to Victory

I could describe other causes of destructive grief, but they would fall into the three categories I've already given: *fear of the unknown* (ignorance of the truth), *idol worship* (accepting non-truth), or *skepticism* (rejecting the truth). Anything that cuts you off from the gospel truth cuts off your life, as you slide into the anguish and lethargy of grief. But when you accept the gospel truth, you open a channel that God can use to deliver a victory.

Charlotte Sanford suffered a rare eye disease called *posterior uveitis*. Doctors at the Mayo Clinic said there was no hope for her condition; she would gradually go blind. But one day her children were wrestling in the living room and one of them accidentally scratched the eye of her son Pete; Charlotte and her husband rushed him to an eye specialist. The doctor soon took care of Pete's minor injury, then turned to Charlotte. "How long has it been since your last eye exam?" he asked.

"About fifteen years," she said. She told him about the barrage of eye tests she'd had then, and the discouraging prognosis the examiners had given her.

"Fifteen years is a long time," the doctor finally said. "We've learned a lot that we never knew before. Would you let me test your eyes again?"

She reluctantly agreed. Five hours later, the doctor compiled all the results. "Your right eye is completely blind," he said.

"But the left eye might be saved, if we can remove the scar tissue with surgery." If the surgery failed, she might lose what little sight was left.

As Charlotte left his office, she pondered what the Lord would have her do.

Throughout the years of my growing blindness I had learned that the most important thing to bear in mind as I prayed was: "Thy will be done. . . ." To me [those words] simply meant that I should want what God wants, rather than asking God to perform for me what I want.[3]

On a later visit, the doctor told Charlotte that he would attempt the surgery if she wanted to take the risk. She agreed. After four hours of surgery and many weeks of uncertainty behind the bandages, Charlotte opened her eyes and saw a fuzzy, jumbled world. With the aid of special glasses, she regained most of her sight in the one eye. She says:

. . .It was a miracle that restored my sight—not the spectacular, instantaneous cure generally thought of as miraculous, but a genuine miracle nonetheless.

It was Jesus, I know, Who led me to a doctor who had had special experience with my own rare eye problem. And it was Jesus Who guided that doctor's hands as he opened the world to me once again.[4]

Charlotte had every earthly reason to give up. Even after the surgery, most people would have felt discouraged and impatient to see. But Charlotte knew she was in the Lord's hands and He would do what was best for her—even if that meant losing her eyesight. She accepted that. She surrendered to the truth of God's sovereign power, and then He healed her.

REDEMPTIVE GRIEF

Now let us look at several types of redemptive grief. The key difference between destructive grief and redemptive grief is *our attitude toward the situation* that grieves us. The feelings in both kinds of grief are much the same. But when we put those feelings to good use, God turns the grief into a miracle and makes it redemptive.

Godly Sorrow

One kind of redemptive grief is *sorrow for our sin.* Look again at the verse of Scripture from 2 Corinthians, which I quoted in the first chapter. But this time notice the verses that precede and follow it:

Second Corinthians 7:9—*"Now I rejoice, not that ye were made sorry, but that ye sorrowed to repentance. . . ."* Here Paul refers to the sorrow felt by the Christians at Corinth after they received a particularly strong letter from him. Paul had criticized the Christians at Corinth because they tolerated immorality, church fights, and disorderly worship services. Paul's young helper Titus told him that the Corinthians had taken the letter to heart and had repented of their sin.

". . . For ye were made sorry after a godly manner, that ye might receive damage by us in nothing." What does Paul mean by "damage"? He means that the Christians at Corinth did not let their grief destroy them. The letter made them feel sorry, but they did not become bitter toward Paul or argue about who was at fault. They fell on their knees and repented. They dealt with the problem. They confessed their sin and asked God to forgive them.

Verse 10—*"For godly sorrow worketh repentance to salvation not to be repented of: but the sorrow of the world worketh death.''* I like what the Jamieson-Fausset-Brown commentary says at this point. Sorrow itself is not repentance, but godly sorrow "tends to repentance."[5] A person has not repented until he *turns away* from sin. The Corinthians were terribly sorry for the wrong things they had done, and they didn't stop with just being sorry. They put immoral people out of the church, settled their disputes, and restored order in their worship services. They repented of their sin—the best result of godly sorrow.

Verse 11—*"For behold . . . what carefulness it wrought in you, yea, what clearing of yourselves. . . ."* Other translations say the Corinthians had "diligence" (NKJB–NT) or "earnestness" (RSV, NASB) to clear themselves. In other words, their sorrow for sin made them knuckle down to the hard business of rooting sin out of their lives.

". . . What indignation . . ." Confronted with a fault, an angry person attacks someone else to defend his integrity. An *indignant* person attends to himself and says, "What a mess! What can I do to change it?"

". . . What fear . . ." The Corinthians feared the disgrace that was sure to come upon the church if they persisted in sin. They feared the known consequences of sin.

". . . Yea, what vehement desire, yea, what zeal, yea, what revenge!" The moment they realized their wrongdoing, they set out to correct it. They would not rest until they put this ungodliness out of the assembly of the saints. How often do we discover a problem in the church and then sit back, waiting to see who'll move to correct it? Not the people in Corinth!

". . . In all things ye have approved yourselves to be clear in this matter." Here the word *approved* literally means "proved" (RSV, NKJB–NT) or "demonstrated" (NASB). The Corinthians' swift action proved they were serious about their repentance. They did not delegate the problems to a committee. They did not say, "Why don't we make a study of this?" When the Lord

convicted their hearts, they got cracking. They purged the sin, and the church survived.

Working to Repentance

Godly sorrow for sin leads to repentance. The preceding passage shows it's true of a church, but what of individuals?

The apostles Peter and John prayed for a lame man at the Beautiful Gate of Jerusalem and saw him healed before their very eyes. The man leaped up and began praising God. The Jews marveled at this, and they ran after the two Christians "greatly wondering" (Acts 3:11). I'm sure the Jews wondered whether there might be something to this Christian gospel after all!

"Ye men of Israel," Peter said, "why marvel ye at this? or why look ye so earnestly on us, as though by our own power or holiness we had made this man to walk? The God of Abraham, and of Isaac, and of Jacob . . . hath glorified his Son Jesus. . . . And his name through faith in his name hath made this man strong . . . (Acts 3:12,13,16).

"Repent ye therefore," he said, "and be converted, that your sins may be blotted out, when the times of refreshing shall come from the presence of the Lord" (Acts 3:19).

We find another example of godly sorrow in Acts 8, which tells about a sorcerer named Simon. On the mission field I have seen witch doctors at work, so I know what a powerful influence they exert. But I have also seen these people converted through the preaching of the gospel, and I know that they usually become God's most potent witnesses. That's what happened to Simon. Scripture says the people of Samaria marveled at Simon's magic and said, "This man is the great power of God" (Acts 8:10). Then the apostle Philip came to town and preached the message of Jesus Christ. People flocked to hear Philip's message; they were converted and baptized. Simon was so amazed at the miracles God wrought at Philip's hand that he believed the gospel, too, and was baptized.

Soon the apostles at Jerusalem heard about the revival in Samaria, so they sent Peter and John to help in the great campaign. I can just imagine what they found: Hundreds of people lined up to be baptized, crippled men throwing their crutches into the air, and the famed magician Simon sitting at the feet of the preacher. The activity was quite a sight! So Peter and John joined in the work. They laid their hands on the new converts and prayed for them to be filled with the Holy Spirit.

The Bible does not really say what happened to the people who received the Holy Spirit on this occasion, but obviously the Spirit gave these new Christians special gifts for their ministry—gifts that set them apart from the unconverted Jews. Simon grew excited when he saw this. He rushed up to the apostles with an offer to buy some Holy-Spirit power for himself. He thought he could induce the Spirit to give him powers, just as he had summoned Satan's power with black magic.

"Thy money perish with thee," Peter snapped, "because thou hast thought that the gift of God may be purchased with money. . . . Thy heart is not right in the sight of God. Repent therefore of this thy wickedness, and pray God, if perhaps the thought of thine heart may be forgiven thee" (Acts 8:20–22).

Peter rebuked Simon's wicked attempt to bribe the Holy Spirit. Simon stood there with the purse in his hand, the proposition on his lips. Everyone could see that he had sinned in word and deed.

But Peter rebuked Simon's secret sin as well. He exhorted Simon to seek God's forgiveness for "the thought of thine heart." Peter knew that Simon had ulterior motives in his request, and those motives were even more wicked than bribery. "I perceive that thou art in the gall of bitterness, and in the bond of iniquity" (v. 23). In other words, he said, "Simon, you can fool some of the people some of the time—but you can't fool God! You'd better repent of your hidden sin, too."

Simon was cut to the quick. He knew Peter was right. He said, "Pray ye to the Lord for me, that none of these things which ye have spoken come upon me" (v. 24). That's godly sorrow. The Bible does not tell us whether Simon followed through to repent from his sin, but at least he called upon God for help. He had the right idea.

These two examples remind us that God may inflict sorrow upon a godly person if he disobeys. The Jews at the Beautiful Gate thought they were true to God; Simon thought he was true to God. But in both cases, the people were wrong. God grieved their hearts with guilt. He shamed them into doing what was right. His methods here do not fit the preconceived notion that many people have of God; they think God is always reassuring and sugary-sweet. When one of God's children wanders away from the truth, God will discipline him. He will convict the heart. Then the disobedient child is the one who must decide whether to repent or to go on with his rebellion. At that point grief becomes redemptive or destructive.

Burdens For Others

Another kind of redemptive grief is *sorrow for the sin of others*. The Bible tells us of several people who sorrowed over the sins of their nation or family and prayed that God would spare them.

The priest Samuel anointed Saul as the first king of Israel. When Saul disobeyed God, sparing the enemy that God told him to destroy, God told Samuel that He was sorry he had made Saul the king. ". . . And it grieved Samuel; and he cried unto the Lord all night" (1 Sam. 15:11). Now, Samuel had done nothing wrong; he had obeyed God with regard to Saul. He

87

sorrowed because he cared about what happened to the king. The Bible says that after this night in prayer, Samuel met Saul and condemned his sin (vv. 12–34). This was the last time he counseled with Saul, "nevertheless Samuel mourned for Saul" (1 Sam. 15:35).

It's interesting to speculate what might have happened if Saul had paid attention to Samuel. If the king had repented, God might have used him to accomplish great things. But we will never know, because Saul "rejected the word of the LORD" (1 Sam. 15:26).

Paul often grieved for the sins of others. When he visited the city of Philippi, for example, a demon-possessed girl followed him through the streets. The demon inside her knew Paul and caused her to say, "These men are the servants of the most high God, which shew unto us the way of salvation" (Acts 16:17). The girl's condition "grieved" Paul (v. 18); he turned around and commanded the demon to come out.

In his letter to the Romans, Paul said he had "great heaviness and continual sorrow in my heart" for the Jews (Rom. 9:2), because he saw so many of them rejecting the gospel. "I could wish that myself were accursed from Christ for my brethren, my kinsmen according to the flesh," he said (v. 3). In other words, if he had the power to choose, he would die without the gospel so that his Jewish friends could hear it and be saved. However, they had to accept or reject Christ for themselves. Paul could only pray for and witness to them.

I know exactly how he felt, because I carry a similar burden for America. This nation needs God. It is being destroyed by divorce, alcoholism, immorality, and so many other ungodly things. I weep for America. I rise about 4:30 each morning to pray for the lost souls of this nation. I've learned that I must turn that burden over to the Lord when I begin the day, or I will be dragged down into despair.

This kind of godly grief motivates a person to act. It compelled Samuel to challenge the king. It compelled Paul to preach the gospel to his Jewish friends. It compels me to reach as many people as I can through radio and television, spreading the news that Jesus came to save them. It may compel you to tell your mate or your children or someone else about the Lord. Make no mistake: Jesus is the One who gives you this burden. He's the One who will redeem another person's life if you act on the burden.

The Grief of Persecution

Still another kind of redemptive grief is *grief under persecution*. When the apostles first preached the gospel in Jerusalem, the Jewish officials threw them in prison. An angel of God released them. The Jews arrested them again, tried them before the Sanhedrin, beat them, and ordered them to stop preaching about Jesus. "And they departed from the presence of the council," Scripture says, "rejoicing that they were counted worthy to suffer shame for his name" (Acts 5:41).

Are you happy to be put to shame for Jesus' sake? Are you glad when the people at your factory or office make fun of your Christian faith? Or do you turn sour toward God? I know being persecuted is not easy. Being laughed at or criticized hurts. But if you continue as a Christian in spite of the persecution, God will turn your sorrow into victory.

Tuberculosis threatened to kill me when I was a teen-ager. The doctors gave up hope, but my godly mother didn't. She kept praying that I would give my life to the Lord. That's exactly what happened, too. On my sickbed I accepted Him as my Savior and promised that I would become a preacher if He healed me. Right away, the tuberculosis vanished.

I went to my father, who was eating breakfast before leaving for his job at the machine shop. "I am going out to preach," I said. "I've promised the Lord that I'll enter the ministry. I've got to leave home."

My father glared at me. He wasn't a Christian, so he cursed me and said, "You can't leave home. You'll starve to death."

He left for work, and I returned to my bedroom. There I slumped on the floor and poured out my grief to the Lord. *Why did you let this happen to me?* I wondered. Suddenly I felt Him tell me to look at Isaiah 41:10,11. I was a new Christian, so I had no idea what those verses said. But I opened my Bible and found the text, which read:

> Fear thou not; for I am with thee: be not dismayed; for I am thy God: I will strengthen thee; yea, I will help thee; yea, I will uphold thee with the right hand of my righteousness. Behold, all they that were incensed against thee shall be ashamed and confounded: they shall be as nothing; and they that strive with thee shall perish.

Let me tell you, my grief turned to joy! My tears turned into laughter. The lump in my throat was gone. The burden on my shoulders was lifted. I was free!

That day I left my home to become a boy evangelist; I never returned. Sure, I've had some disappointments along the way, and I have often carried burdens for other people. But Christ is my Burden-bearer.

If you are a Christian, I'm sure you know the meaning of "suffering shame for the name" of Jesus Christ. Let me encourage you to turn that shame over to Him. Thank Him for it. Praise Him for the privilege of persecution. Then watch how He uses it to bring honor to His name.

YOU CAN'T DO IT YOURSELF

Satan wants you to think you can handle grief on your own.

He wants you to believe that grief is just a mid-life mood change, a dip in your biorhythm, or an unhappy alignment of the planets. If you can find the right formula or analyze your psyche a bit better, he says, you can snap yourself out of it.

That's an insidious lie.

A man walked into a doctor's office and said, "You've got to help me, doctor. I'm dying of sadness. My heart is so full of melancholy that I don't know what to do."

"I know what you need to do," the doctor replied. "You know the circus that's playing in town? I went there last night and saw a clown who cheered everybody up. He's the funniest guy I've ever seen. Go to the circus tonight and see that clown. Believe me, you'll lose your sadness."

The man looked up with doleful eyes and said, "Doctor, I am that clown."

No one can cure his own grief. The task is impossible. The more you try to cheer yourself and work your way out of sorrow, the more despondent and blue you find yourself. At its core, the human heart is sinful and self-destructive. The more you look within yourself for a cure for sadness, the more you find reason for grief.

The same is true of physical healing. A heart surgeon may perform hundreds of operations on other people, but if the surgeon himself ever needs a bypass operation, he must put himself in the hands of another doctor. He cannot save himself.

While I was serving as a missionary in Tibet, I was stricken with Oriental dysentery. This deadly disease causes massive bleeding of the bowels. I can still remember the day I lay down on a lonely Tibetan hillside, weak from the loss of blood. My native guide said I would be dead within thirty-six hours.

In no way could I heal myself. I had no medical knowledge to speak of; I was stranded many miles from the nearest hospital or clinic. My only hope was that the Lord would perform a miracle.

So I prayed, and the Lord healed me again.

So many modern self-help books claim that you can make yourself anything you want to be. They say that if you tell yourself you're a friendly person, you'll become friendly. If you tell yourself you're courageous, you'll be courageous. They say that if you assert yourself, you can overcome any problem. But you cannot pull yourself up by your bootstraps when you are entangled in self-pity, worry, and timidness. You need help from the outside; you need Someone who can free you from that grief.

I am inspired by the story of the Russian dissident Alexander Solzhenitsyn, a Christian who challenged the brutal policies of the Soviet government. Mr. Solzhenitsyn suffered all kinds of insults at the hands of his government and finally was exiled from his native land. Instead of trying to "cheer himself up" with pop psychology or humanistic philosophy, Solzhenitsyn clung to his faith in God. That faith brought him through persecution. Professor Niels C. Nielsen, Jr., comments that "Solzhenitsyn's moral sense led him back to God, not just an idea, but to the living God of history and personal experience.[6]

Of course, many people try the way of self-analysis. They think they can find the answer to all their problems if they just study themselves more carefully and sort out the snarled web of their id, ego, and superego.

This idea has created quite a gaggle of pop psychology cults. Transcendental Meditation is popular in Western countries because it offers self-discovery through meditation. If you sit alone in an incense-filled room and chant your mantra over and over again, you're supposed to "get in touch" with yourself. Werner Erhard's "est" program promises the same thing through yelling and cursing. Even in Christian circles, some counselors are exhorting their people to "self-discovery" instead of searching God's Word for answers.

The Bible tells us not to expect any help from simple self-analysis. In fact, Scripture says this method of problem-solving will make your grief worse, not better. "And I gave my heart to know wisdom, and to know madness and folly: I perceived that this also is vexation of spirit. For in much wisdom is much grief: and he that increaseth knowledge increaseth sorrow" (Eccl. 1:17,18).

Here King Solomon says that all of his wise self-understanding did not bring him peace but only vexed his heart more. When he probed his own depths, he realized how truly weak he was. He uncovered the folly of human self-conceit.

Socrates said, "The unexamined life is not worth living." Shakespeare wrote, "To thine own self be true: and it shall follow as night the day, thou canst be false to no man." Despite these catchy phrases, the utter despair that proceeds from self-knowledge can drive a person to ruin.

The basic idea of self-analysis is that you are wise enough to know what's wrong and how to make it right. The other key principle is that you have sufficient will to do this.

Both of these ideas are dead wrong.

A young oil company executive named Keith Miller found out how wrong they were. An auto accident while he was in college nearly cost him his life. While he lay there beside the highway with a broken neck, he felt the peace of God envelop him. He thought, *What a shame to learn about this kind of peace so late in life!*

As it turned out, God spared Keith's life, and the young man soon pushed all thought of God out of his mind again. He scrambled to make the grade in college and get a well-paying job. He learned to assert himself on the job and to make subordinates snap to his command. Still, something was missing. Keith resigned his job and entered seminary. He suspected that somehow he could find peace with God, so he set out to learn all about the great theological ideas of the ages. He scrambled to make the grade again. Still, there was no peace.

He dropped out of seminary and returned to his old job. He remembers:

> There seemed to be no hope, no ultimate purpose, anymore.
> . . I used to walk down the streets and suddenly would break out in a cold sweat. I thought I might be losing my mind. One day it was so bad that I got in my company car and drove off on a field trip alone. As I was driving through the tall pine woods country of East Texas I suddenly pulled up beside the road and stopped. I remember sitting there in complete despair. I had always been an optimistic person, and had always had the feeling that there was "one more bounce in the ball." . . . But now there was no tomorrow in my situation. I was like a man on a great gray treadmill going no place, in a world that was made up of black, black clouds all around me.
>
> As I sat there I began to weep like a little boy, which I suddenly realized I was inside. I looked toward the sky. There was nothing I wanted to do with my life. And I said, "God, if there's anything you want in this stinking soul, take it."[7]

Here we have a perfect picture of the man who tries to master his own grief. Keith had achieved everything he set out to do. He was successful by every earthly measure, but he had no peace. He explored his inner self and found that he was but a "little boy." A spoiled kid was calling the shots in his life, and that's enough to drive anyone to despair.

As soon as he surrendered his life to God, Keith felt a burden lift from his shoulders. When he threw away his selfish ambition, God gave him the zeal to serve only Him. Keith Miller found a whole new purpose for his life. He said, "It *is* like being born again."[8]

When Keith Miller learned who he really was, he was sorry. That sorrow moved him to repent and brought him to God. Such self-analysis is the only kind that does any good. The Bible says, "Examine yourselves, whether ye be in the faith; prove your own selves. Know ye not your own selves, how that Jesus

Christ is in you, except ye be reprobates?" (2 Cor. 13:5). Search your heart—not to learn what a wonderful, mature person you are, but to learn whether Jesus Christ has control of your life. See if you find Jesus Christ inside. If not, ask Him to come in, because He's the only One who can make your life worth living.

THE CHOICE IS YOURS

Yes, grief is volatile. It can bring relief and healing, or it can inflict terrible destruction, depending on what we do with it.

God offers you the power to conquer grief and let it change your life for the better. To find that power, you need to turn your grief over to Him. When you feel sorrow, fear, guilt, or any other kind of grief, ask Him what is wrong with your life. Let Him show you what to do about it. Then obey Him, and He can give you the victory.

If you are willing, He is able.

NOTES

1. Will and Ariel Durant, *The Lessons of History* (New York: Simon and Schuster, 1969), pp. 42, 43.
2. Maurice Rawlings, *Beyond Death's Door* (Nashville: Thomas Nelson Publishers, 1978), p. 24.
3. Charlotte Sanford, "The Woman Who Dared Not Cry," *Guideposts*, December 1979, p. 19.
4. Ibid., p. 24.
5. Robert Jamieson, A. R. Fausset, and David Brown, *Commentary on the Whole Bible* (Grand Rapids, Mich.: Zondervan Publishing House, 1961), p. 1244.
6. Niels C. Nielsen, Jr., *Solzhenitsyn's Religion* (Nashville: Thomas Nelson Publishers, 1975), p. 140.
7. Keith Miller, *A Taste of New Wine* (Waco, Tex.: Word Books, 1965), pp. 38,39.
8. Ibid., p. 39.

6

ANTIDOTES FOR GRIEF'S POISON

A two-year-old child swallows a fistful of Drano and starts to cry. Mother rushes into the kitchen, sees the problem, and calls the Poison Control Center. "Give him milk immediately," says a voice on the other end. "Then rush him to the emergency room."

Similar scenes are repeated in hundreds of different homes every day. The antidote may not clear the child of all danger, but it does prevent serious harm until further help is available.

In this chapter, I want to give you some antidotes to destructive grief. Like chemical antidotes, these ideas may not clear you of all trouble, but they will help prevent damage until you can get to the One who will cure your grief. (We'll talk about Him in Chapter 9.) We have seen that grief is a poison that can destroy your peace of mind, your happiness, and your very life. Grief also can disrupt your relationship with God and undermine your human friendships and family ties. You need to know how to counteract the dangers of grief. Here are some ideas for first aid:

MAKE A PEACEFUL ENVIRONMENT

Family counselor Dr. Craig Massey, who regularly conducts seminars on family living, advises parents to let each child have an "Isle of Tranquility"—a place and time reserved for that person alone, without distractions or interruptions. Maybe the place is the living room sofa, where the teen-aged son can nap for an hour after school. Or the "isle" might be an extension phone in the den, where the daughter can talk for an hour with her friends without being hassled. Wherever it is, that place and time set apart is important to the well-being of a child.

The same is true of adults. Each one of us needs a place where we can withdraw from the demands of job and family, just to meditate or to engage in some creative work. My study is such a place for me. We have a lovely home overlooking the hills of suburban South Bend, and I love to spend an hour just before dawn in my study, meditating on God's Word and praying at the window. The family knows this time is set apart. I take neither phone calls nor visits (and at that hour I seldom get any). I have a place where I can gather my thoughts before the day begins.

Setting aside such a time for the whole family is just as important. Pick at least one night a week when everyone agrees not to schedule a ball game, sales meeting, or bowling date. Set aside that night for some quiet activity together as a family— preferably something that will give you a chance for face-to-face conversation. A table game, a craft project, or reading and discussing a book together are some ideas you might try.

One morning as Dr. Norman Vincent Peale ate breakfast with a couple of men, he asked, "How did you sleep last night?"

"I felt just about as tired when I got up as I did when I went to bed," one man replied. "I think I should stop listening to the news just before I go to sleep. Last night I got an earful of trouble."

"Well, I had a wonderful night," the other man said. "I get all my news from the evening paper, and put it aside well before I'm ready to retire.

"I used to be very nervous, high-strung, and tense," he explained. "Then it occurred to me that I had never seen these characteristics in my father. He was a quiet, active, sturdy man up to the day he died at age eighty-five. The doctor said his heart was as good as if he'd been a man of forty."

Dr. Peale and the other man raised their eyebrows.

"Every evening at nine o'clock," the man said, "my father gathered his children around him, sat down in an old rocking chair, put on his glasses, and read to us out of the Bible. Then he prayed. I can still feel the sense of confidence and moral cleanness that all of us had when we trooped off to bed.

"When I left home, I decided that was an old-fashioned custom," he said. "I gave it up. But now we have gone back to it. I gather my wife and two kids around me, and we read from the same old Book my father used. And I go to bed with a mind full of peace."[1]

You too can have a mind full of peace if you create an environment of peace. Make yourself a special place where you can shut out the world and its pressures. Agree with yourself and your family that you will set aside this time for calm and creativity. It will make a tremendous difference in the way you handle your grief.

Jesus showed His disciples that they needed this. "And he said unto them, Come ye yourselves apart into a desert place, and rest a while: for there were many coming and going, and they had no leisure so much as to eat" (Mark 6:31). He knew the demands of their ministry would overwhelm them if they did not take time for peace and quietness. Times of testing lay ahead.

Jesus Himself often tried to withdraw into a quiet place where He could pray and meditate. At times He was not successful, because the people found Him and thronged around Him again (Luke 4:42). But on the night He was betrayed and arrested, He went into the Garden of Gethsemane to pray alone. "My soul is exceeding sorrowful unto death," He told his disciples. "Tarry ye here, and watch." He then walked beyond them a short distance, fell to the ground, and prayed (Mark 14:34,35). He needed that moment of solitude before facing the grief of His trial and crucifixion.

Youth leader Winkie Pratney says that new Christians should make a special effort to set aside these quiet times:

> . . . Too many words, too much mixing purposelessly with people can take the edge off your spiritual axe. There is nothing more beautiful to the soul than to go off quietly somewhere late in the afternoon, evening or early morning to spend an hour or two with God. . . . Love is sweetened by stillness.[2]

BE HAPPY—
EVEN WHEN YOU DON'T FEEL LIKE IT!

If you were to conduct a man-on-the-street interview in your home town and ask, "What is *happiness*?"—I'd venture to say most would reply, "Well, *happiness* is a feeling that . . ." Then they would explain what they think a happy feeling is. But happiness is not a feeling; it is an *attitude*, a way you set your mind. In fact, to be more basic than that: Happiness is the act of making up your mind to receive whatever comes to you.

Our modern word *happy* comes from the Middle English word *hap*, which means "occurrence" or "incident." We get our modern words *happen, perhaps,* and *haphazard* from that same word. This should tip us off to what *happy* really means. Let me suggest a few definitions:

- *Happen*—To occur or come about. Example: "Look what *happened* to me!"
- *Perhaps*—Resulting from a thing that may occur or come about. Example: "If *perhaps* you find my wallet, I hope you'll return it."
- *Haphazard*—To occur or come about by chance

("hazard"). Example: "You have a *haphazard* way of following a map!"

● *Happy*—To accept or adjust to what occurs. Example: "I'm *happy* I failed my driver's test, because I need more walking exercise."

Do you think I'm making this up? Then notice how a standard dictionary defines the word:

> *happy*—(1) favored by luck or fortune: FORTUNATE; (2) notably well adapted or fitting: FELICITOUS; (3) enjoying well-being and contentment: JOYOUS; . . . .[3]

Notice that the word describes how you *respond* to what comes your way (what "happens"). The meaning is you have adjusted well; you have accepted your lot with joy. The opposite of *happy* is the word *hapless*, which means "unfortunate" or "ruined by what happens."

My point is this: Our society assumes that happiness is a matter of how you *feel*, but it is really a matter of how you *act*.

It's not unusual for someone to come up to me and say, "Brother Sumrall, I'm so *happy*!" I feel like saying, "Are you really? Or do you just *feel* happy?" I know that next week the same person is likely to come back and say, "Oh, Brother Sumrall! What a terrible week I've had! I'm not happy anymore." That kind of person rides an emotional roller coaster, always up and down, without ever being truly happy. That kind of person cannot adjust to what happens.

Dr. Robert Schuller tells of making a South Pacific cruise during which the ship had to navigate through dangerous coral reefs. When a special pilot came on board to guide the ship, a crowd gathered on deck to watch him direct the boat through the menacing shoals. Someone said nervously, "We're drawing twenty-nine feet of water, and the channel is only thirty-one feet deep.''

A fearful hush fell across the group. They expected to hear the grinding noise of collision at any minute.

Then another tourist piped up, "Why, that's two feet to spare! And we're only going seventeen knots . . . We think nothing of riding in a car at fifty-five miles an hour, with another car coming toward us at the same speed, and only two feet of dividing line between us!"

The crowd laughed. He was right. That simple glimpse of truth put the danger in perspective again, and they were able to enjoy the ride.[4]

Being able to put what happens in its proper perspective is an important key to happiness. You must learn to take happenings in stride. Then you really will be happy, and grief cannot drag you down.

BE GOD'S "WATER BOY"

Jesus said, ". . . Whosoever drinketh of the water that I shall give him shall never thirst; but the water that I shall give him shall be in him a well of water springing up into everlasting life" (John 4:14). He wants every one of us to carry His "living water" to people dying of grief.

Every Christian knows that. But here's something that most people don't know: *The water boy never goes thirsty!* If you lift the grief of the people around you, you'll find that grief loses its power over *you!* Keep carrying the "water of life" that comes from Jesus Christ, and you will never run dry yourself.

Dawson Trotman drove heavy-duty equipment at a lumberyard in California when he first became a Christian. God used him there to carry the gospel to people who were depressed and hopeless about life. One of his friends later said, "The whole town knew it. He told everyone he saw. He would corner you any place and say, 'Have you heard what's happened to me?' "[5]

Over the next three decades, Dawson worked at several different jobs, always sharing his Lord wherever he went. He founded a cluster of ministries to reach high school students, soldiers, sailors, and businessmen. Billy Graham asked him to design the follow-up program that became a key part of the Graham crusades. No matter how busy Dawson was, though, he always had time to share a word of Scripture and challenge someone to accept the Lord. When Billy Graham preached at Dawson's funeral in 1956, he said:

> Dawson was a man with a *consuming passion for souls.* His love for the lost coupled with his boundless energy took him to the ends of the world to encourage, train, and strengthen laborers in Christ's vineyard. I remember seeing him in these meetings, talking with individuals, making appointments all day long to help people grow in the grace and knowledge of Jesus Christ. Over in London, many times in the counseling room he and my wife would be the last ones dealing with people. . . .[6]

God gave Dawson Trotman an amazing reserve of physical strength to do the work of witnessing. He carried Dawson through some very discouraging times as he formed those ministries. But because Dawson was willing to be God's "water boy," God kept him from being discouraged.

Sharing the "water" does not always mean leading a person to Christ. Born-again Christians may need the "water" of encouragement or correction to get back on the track of their spiritual lives. Bad news can lay a Christian low. At times like that, you can be the "water boy" who brings that person a refreshing draught from God's Word.

Dr. Schuller gives an interesting example of how God used

him to do this. Lois Wendell, who had been his secretary for two years, phoned him from home one day and awkwardly said, "Bob, I just found out—I've got cancer. It's one of the most virulent types."

Dr. Schuller rushed to her house. He knew she needed some word of encouragement in the face of this awful news. So he knelt beside Lois in her living room and prayed, "O, God, we're so thankful today. We're thankful that we discovered this malignancy at an early stage. We're thankful that we live in a country where the finest and best medical help is available. We're thankful that we're living in a day when great advances are being made in cancer treatment. We're thankful that Lois is surrounded by a vast number of friends. . . ."[7]

Such was the attitude of his prayer. He put in practice 1 Thessalonians 5:18: "In every thing give thanks: for this is the will of God in Christ Jesus concerning you." Sharing Scripture with Lois was not enough; Dr. Schuller practiced it with her. He went as a Christian brother and taught her how to praise God, even in the face of death.

God healed Lois Wendell. She is still alive twelve years later, a living testimony of what God can do through someone who is willing to be His "water boy."

BE AN AMBASSADOR OF HOPE

Every day dozens of people see you or hear your voice. You may not have an opportunity to talk with each one of them, but you can still convey a mood of hope and happiness. Hope is contagious. And as you spread that blessed "infection" to those people, you'll build up a spiritual immunity to grief.

If you work in an office, you should make it your job to create happiness there. Hum a happy song to yourself. Share a funny story with the other employees. Smile. Walk with a sprightly step. Let everything about your actions radiate the joy that you feel inside as a Christian, and you will be surprised how quickly your friends respond.

When you come home at night, decide that you are going to be Mr. or Mrs. Happiness when you walk through the door. Shout a cheerful greeting to your mate. Hug your children. Listen to what they tell you about their day, and take an interest in them. You set the mood of your entire evening in the first three minutes after you enter the house; decide to make a grand entrance every time.

When the phone rings, wait a second before you answer and put yourself in a cheerful frame of mind. Whisper this prayer: "Lord, let me be a blessing to whoever is on the other end of this conversation." Don't wait to see who's calling before you decide whether to be happy; start off on that note. You will find that the other person will respond in kind—even if he or she is in a grouchy mood at the start.

Turn every problem into praise. In other words, show an especially good attitude toward the "problem people" you meet during the day. Say the check-out girl overcharges you; be friendly and patient as you work out the mistake. The world is not accustomed to this kind of behavior, so other folks may seem puzzled at first. Don't get discouraged; you can make a great difference in the way that clerk treats the person after you.

A friend of mine recently mailed his church newsletter and told the postal clerk, "I just want you to know how much I appreciate the work you people do. You always get our newsletter out on time. I'm really amazed how you can handle all of this mail and still deliver it so quickly."

The clerk almost passed out! No one gives the U.S. Postal Service a compliment! She stammered for a moment and then said, "Why, thank you. It's nice to know we're doing something right."

ANTIDOTES TO DEPRESSION

Depression is not a healthy thing for an individual, a family, or a church. Anytime we sulk in our sorrows, we invite depression to come. The Word of God says we have better things to think about. Read Philippians 4:8,9:

"Finally, brethren, whatsoever things are true . . ." It's so much more constructive to think about the good things we *know* will happen, than to shudder at the bad things that *might* happen. Our imaginations concoct some pretty scary things. If we mull over our fears about the future, the fears grow. Better to mull over the good that we know is true.

". . . Whatsoever things are honest . . ." The New King James Bible translates this "noble." The NASB renders it "honorable." You get the basic idea; thinking about something decent and morally uplifting is better than whispering about the latest scandal. The world is full of corruption, but why should we make corruption the topic of our conversation? Why elevate it to the top of our thoughts? Why not focus on the honest, noble, and honorable things happening around us?

". . . Whatsoever things are just . . ." Every one of us has been wronged at one time or another. If we cared to recite all of the unkind things people have said about us, rude things people have done to us, or the offensive rumors that have come back to us, we'd feel pretty depressed! But self-pity does us no good. Rather than thinking about the unjust things that have happened to us, think about the blessings other people have given us. Thank God for the kindness of our neighbors and friends.

". . . Whatsoever things are pure . . ." Our government has spent billions of dollars to rid this land of air pollution, water pollution, noise pollution, and so on. One kind of pollution no government program can solve: thought pollution. Don't allow lust, greed, and hatefulness to pollute your mind.

Clean up your thoughts. Ask God to forgive any impure thoughts that come to mind, and rebuke the unclean spirit that produces them.

"*. . . Whatsoever things are lovely . . .*" We live in a generation of snobs. So often I hear people say, "Isn't that an awful-looking dress?" Or, "What would ever make a person choose that color for a house?" Or, "The food is much better at the restaurant across the street; why did we have to eat here?" They try to prove their "good taste" by criticizing things. Thank God for the lovely table your wife set for supper, the nice card a friend sent to cheer you, the uplifting sermon your pastor gave you last Sunday. It's hard to be depressed when you're thankful!

"*. . . Whatsoever things are of good report . . .*" Here the NASB says, "Whatever is of good repute" or "attractive." In other words, what good things would excite the people you talk with today? Perhaps you should subscribe to some good Christian magazines to counterbalance all the gloom that's served up in your newspaper. Every day people do heroic things; they give sacrificially of themselves to help others. Wherever that happens, we know the Spirit of God is at work. Tell others about those things.

"*. . . If there be any virtue . . .*" Why not tell someone how much you appreciate the *virtue* in his or her life? We think we should send a thank-you note when a person gives us something, but we can also say thank you for what that person is. Say, "I appreciate your patience." Or, "Thank you for listening to me." Or, "I'm so grateful for your tact in that situation." Virtue is its own reward, but it doesn't hurt to add the reward of praise! Which leads us to the last thought:

"*. . . If there be any praise . . .*" When you suffer the death of someone you love, you may feel short-tempered with people. You may not find much to praise in them. But praise will unlock unexpected power in your soul. No matter how clumsy or inadequate people may seem to you just now, they are still created in the image of God. You should be able to find something to praise in them, saying something like, "My, how kind of you to call me!" (even if it is eleven o'clock at night).

These thoughts from God's Word can be a powerful antidote to depression. Apply them daily in your time of grief.

Really, it's not so hard to be an ambassador of hope. Take time to give someone a kind word or a thoughtful gesture, and you will brighten the day for many others. You will also make yourself more able to deal with grief when it comes.

GET TO THE TRUTH

Instead of fearing what lies ahead, investigate what lies ahead. Get the facts. Learn everything you can about the problem before you spend one moment grieving over it. Usually, you will discover the problem is not so big after all. You will save yourself a lot of useless vexation.

If you think you have a serious illness, go to your doctor and let him examine you. I wonder how many people who avoid the doctor because they *might* have a grave disease actually worry themselves into a grave disease. I suspect many do. Knowing the truth about yourself is far better than letting your imagination run wild.

Not long ago a man went to Indianapolis for open heart surgery and asked his doctor his chances of pulling through. "I think you ought to know," the doctor said, "your chances of survival are about five percent."

The patient was relieved. He knew what to expect. He put his family affairs in order, gathered his loved ones around him, and entered the operating room with confidence. This Christian man knew he could expect the worst, so he was prepared for it. (By the way, God brought him through the surgery.)

Plan according to the facts, not according to your fears. Then grief will glance off your back like a silly paper plane. Jesus said, "Ye shall know the truth, and the truth shall make you free" (John 8:32).

It's important, too, to air hidden feelings. Church feuds start because a few hurt feelings were "kept under wraps" until they festered and broke open. Divorce comes from an unwillingness to talk about hurt feelings or the resentment that one partner has for the other. Satan hates honesty, because he likes to work under cover. When the facts are out in the open, setting people against one another is much harder for him.

In a letter to his newlywed son Philip, Charlie Shedd made this observation:

> . . . To let someone into your heart can be plain awful. Sometimes it is scary. It brings up things we didn't know we had, and one of these is resistance. This is the psychological term for slamming the door, running away fast, and saying, "Let's forget the whole business."
>
> This is why so few people have what it takes to make it all the way through to genuine transparency. But you can. . . .[8]

You must work at *transparency*—letting the other person see your real self. That's a painful experience. To make it happen, you must be willing to confess your grudges, your uncertainties, and your reasons for holding back from the other person. But honesty will repel a lot of needless grief away from your life.

HOW TO USE THE ANTIDOTES

If I had time and space, I could list several other antidotes to grief. These examples are only a beginning. Remember that an antidote is not a final cure, so don't rely on these suggestions to overcome grief for you. Only Jesus Christ can do that. However, if you practice these ways of thinking daily, the venom of grief will lose its sting. The ill effects will not destroy you. You will have a chance to get to the Great Physician, who will show you how to conquer grief.

NOTES

1. Norman Vincent Peale, "Getting a Mind Full of Peace" (New York: Sermon Publications, Inc., 1951), pp. 3,4.
2. Winkie Pratney, *A Handbook for Followers of Jesus* (Minneapolis: Bethany Fellowship, Inc., 1977), p. 107.
3. *Webster's Seventh New Collegiate Dictionary* (Springfield, Mass.: G. C. Merriam Company, 1963), p. 378.
4. Robert H. Schuller, *You Can Become the Person You Want to Be* (Old Tappan, N.J.: Spire Books, 1976), p. 112.
5. Betty Lee Skinner, *Daws: The Story of Dawson Trotman* (Grand Rapids, Mich.: Zondervan Publishing House, 1974), p. 31.
6. Ibid., p. 385.
7. Robert H. Schuller, *You Can Become the Person You Want to Be,* p. 113.
8. Charlie W. Shedd, *Letters to Philip* (Old Tappan, N.J.: Spire Books, 1968), p. 28.

7

GRIEF IN THE BIBLE

I am a student of human nature. I like to watch people as they stroll down the street. I notice how young lovers hold hands, how elderly people gesture as they talk, how children fondle a new toy. I love human beings. I am going to live with them in eternity, so I have devoted myself to learning all I can about what makes different people "tick." Along the way, I have seen how grief affects people in different ways.

I have seen grief in the face of a young mother in India, with a starving baby and an empty tin pail, begging for food. I have seen grief in the bent, weary backs of prison work gangs along the railroads of Siberia. I have watched the silent grief of an old widow sitting on the curb in a city square in Brazil, vacantly staring past me. Grief is universal. But some people are better able to handle grief than others.

We see this as we examine cases of grief in the Bible. Some people were so firmly rooted that grief hardly caused a ripple in their lives; others were eaten up by it. Let us consider a few of these cases and see what the Bible reveals about these people's handling of grief.

ADAM AND EVE

As we saw earlier, the first two people on earth knew sorrow and grief. Adam and Eve lost nearly all the privileges they had: They were expelled from paradise, forced to toil for their food, had to bear children in pain, and lost the intimate fellowship they once had with God. They could still talk with God in prayer and offer sacrifices to Him (as their sons Cain and Abel did). But they lost their opportunity to serve God without sin and guilt. Matthew Henry says:

> . . . Sin brought sorrow into the world; . . . [it] made the world a vale of tears, brought showers of trouble upon our heads, and opened the springs of sorrows in our hearts, and so deluged the world: Had we known no guilt, we should have known no grief.[1]

Adam and Eve suffered for their sin. God gave them a choice: *Obey Me and you will live, or disobey Me and you will die.* They chose the latter, and we all feel the pangs of their mistake. We could delve into quite a study of how their original sin has been passed along to us, but for now, let us focus on what sin did to Adam and Eve themselves. How did they suffer as a result of their sin?

The Bible is sketchy about Adam and Eve's life after they left the Garden, but it says that Eve soon bore two sons, Cain and Abel (Gen. 4:1,2). Since God warned that she would bear children in sorrow, Eve obviously suffered pain in giving birth. Imagine how hard this was for her, as no one had ever gone through this before. Eve had no idea what to expect nor could she draw comfort from an experienced friend; she only knew that childbirth would be a sorrowful experience. As some writers have said, childbirth is like a descent into the Valley of Death to bring back the gift of life. Some women don't come back.

But Eve did survive, and her sons grew up. Abel became a shepherd, while Cain was a farmer (see Gen. 4:2). Adam and his sons had to extract their living from the cursed earth, struggling against poor soil, brambles, seasons of drought, and other problems farmers and ranchers have known ever since. The earth did not yield food freely as it had in the Garden of Eden; now man had to struggle for even the most simple living.

They lived in shame. Before they sinned, Genesis 2:25 tells us, Adam and Eve were naked but "not ashamed." After they sinned, however, they sewed together fig leaves to hide their nakedness. They were embarrassed to let God see them. They no longer were a natural part of His creation, good in every way; now they were rebellious and perverse. They were ashamed to admit who they were.

Pain, struggle, and shame—such was the daily lot of Adam and Eve. Adam lived to the age of nine hundred thirty. We cannot imagine how anyone could live that long, but reasonably thinking they must have suffered the physical impairments of age. We groan to think what our bodies may be like if we live to age ninety-three or one hundred three; but what if we lived to nine hundred thirty? The aches and pains would be indescribable. Also remember that this couple bore Seth when they were one hundred years old, and more "sons and daughters" after that (Gen. 5:3,4). How would it be to run a nursery at that ripe old age?

Did Adam and Eve repent of their sin? The Bible does not record any further rebellion against God on their part. Perhaps they learned their severe lesson and turned away from sin. Perhaps they devoted themselves to the Lord from that point on. We do not know.

Nor do we know whether Adam and Eve became bitter toward God. The Bible is silent here. It does say that Cain and Abel offered sacrifices to God (see Gen. 4:3,4), and when grandson Enos was born men began "to call upon the name of the LORD" (Gen. 4:26). This suggests that Adam and Eve tried to guide their family in the way of the Lord.

The entire episode of Adam and Eve's fall from grace is a sad affair which separated them from God and eventually brought their deaths. They were the world's first victims of grief.

JOSEPH

This young man was a dreamer, in the best sense of the word. When he was just seventeen, Joseph dreamed of a day when he would have a place of honor and his family would bow down to him (see Gen. 37:2ff). Many youths have dreamed of greatness, but Joseph went one step further: He told his family about it. They laughed. His father rebuked him, and his brothers harbored a grudge against him. The first time they found Joseph alone, his brothers wrestled him to the ground and would have killed him if the eldest had not intervened. They sold him into slavery instead (which in those days was hardly better than death).

This series of events was enough to grieve any person, but Joseph did not let circumstances get the best of him. He began working his way up the chain of command in his master's house in Egypt. He became overseer of all the household. Then one day, while the master was gone, the lady of the house tried to seduce Joseph. He refused, and she had him thrown into prison.

For the second time, Joseph was "at the bottom of the heap." But he did not let it get the best of him. He began working for advancement in the jail, and the head jailer made him chief trustee. Joseph had authority over all the prisoners.

Two prisoners—a baker and a cup bearer—came to Joseph for interpretation of their dreams. Joseph told the cup bearer he was about to be restored to the king's court, but he told the baker he would lose his head. He asked the cup bearer to remember him when he returned to the king's favor. Three days later, Joseph's predictions were fulfilled. The baker went to the gallows, and the cup bearer went to the king's table—and promptly forgot about Joseph.

Joseph was a three-time loser! All of the circumstances indicated he was going to be caged in that hell-hole for the rest of his life. Yet Joseph kept on doing his job, waiting and trusting that his childhood vision would come true, because he knew it was from the Lord.

Two years passed. Then Pharaoh himself had a troubling dream, and he asked his wise men to interpret it. They couldn't. Only then did the cup bearer remember his promise to Joseph, and he told Pharaoh about that strange Hebrew slave who could tell the meaning of dreams. Pharaoh summoned Joseph from prison. Joseph deciphered his dream and warned him to prepare for seven years of famine. Pharaoh discerned that he was right, and said:

> . . . Forasmuch as God hath shewed thee all this, there is none so discreet and wise as thou art: thou shalt be over my house, and according unto thy word shall all my people be ruled: only in the throne will I be greater than thou (Gen. 41:39,40).

Since Joseph's former master was an officer of Pharaoh, I well imagine that he was a guest at Joseph's inauguration ceremony. I suppose the officer's wife sat there trembling, thinking to herself, *As soon as we get through eating he'll have my head cut off*. Joseph had the power to do that, but the Bible does not show him taking vengeance on Potiphar's wife. I suspect his attitude toward her was much like that toward his own brothers when they came to Egypt to buy grain. He fell on their necks and kissed them, inviting them to bring their families into the land. Even as he lay on his deathbed many years later, Joseph did not strike back at his persecutors. He said, ". . . Ye thought evil against me; but God meant it unto good, to bring to pass, as it is this day, to save much people alive" (Gen. 50:20).

Joseph saw God working in situations that were grievous, so he was patient. He did not complain; he just continued doing God's will, waiting for the fulfillment of God's plan.

114

HANNAH

First Samuel 1 tells about the grief of Hannah, wife of Elkanah. As was customary in those days, Elkanah had another wife as well; her name was Peninnah. This second wife bore him several children, while Hannah was barren.

The Bible says that Elkanah loved Hannah so much that he gave her the same portions of food that he gave to Peninnah and her children. But infertility was a great shame among the Jewish people for they believed it showed God's disfavor.

Each year Hannah went up to the temple to pray that she would bear a son. Some people would think it bold enough to ask God for a child—any child—but Hannah asked for the best possible blessing: a son. The right of inheritance passed through the son.

The Bible says, "And she, greatly distressed, prayed to the LORD and wept bitterly" (1 Sam. 1:10 NASB). Hannah did not accuse God of neglecting her, but she did not give up praying, either. She was sorely grieved because of the situation, and I'm sure she was tempted to turn against God. But she didn't. She kept praying and trusting Him for an answer.

The high priest Eli saw her lips moving in fervent prayer and thought she was drunk. He rebuked her for being intoxicated in the temple. But she said, "No, my lord, I am a woman of a sorrowful spirit: I have drunk neither wine nor strong drink, but have poured out my soul before the LORD. . . . for out of the abundance of my complaint ["great concern" NASB; "great anxiety" RSV] and grief have I spoken hitherto" (vv. 15,16).

Notice what Hannah did with her grief. She spilled it out before the Lord in prayer. She did not try to pretend that she felt nothing; nor did she murmur to her friends about how cruel God was. She took the problem straight to the Lord, pleading for an answer. Surely this is a constructive use of grief.

Eli blessed Hannah and prayed that the Lord would grant

what she asked for. Hannah then left the temple, broke her fast, "and her countenance was no more sad" (v. 18). She knew how to leave her burden with the Lord.

Within a year, Hannah bore her husband a son and named him *Samuel* ("heard of God"). The boy's very name reminded everyone of the fact that God had heard Hannah's prayer in her grief and answered it. The boy took priestly training under Eli and became one of the greatest prophets of Israel.

Hannah's grief came of unfulfilled desire. Millions of people suffer that same malady today—grieving over children they want to bear, jobs they want to secure, mates they want to marry, and so on. Hannah gives us a good example of what to do with this kind of grief. We should take it to the Lord in prayer, surrender it to Him, then wait upon His time to answer our plea. We can be confident that He will hear and answer according to His will.

DAVID

God may not answer our prayer in quite the way we expect. David's experience is a good illustration of this.

As you know, David was a shepherd boy who loved to play music on his harp. He wrote some of the most beautiful song-poems in history, recorded in the Book of Psalms. These songs reflect the wide range of moods that David knew as shepherd, soldier, and finally king of Israel. The mood of grief is a recurring theme.

David had many things to grieve about. His king was jealous of him because he had killed the giant Goliath. Even though King Saul invited David to become his court musician, he was always plotting to kill the lad. Saul would fly into violent fits of rage and throw his spear at David while the boy was playing for him. This must have troubled David's heart. Saul's jealousy threatened the ties between David and Jonathan, Saul's son and

David's closest friend. When David fled from the king, Saul tried to learn his whereabouts from Jonathan. They waged a constant battle of wits.

When Saul died and David became the king, he faced enemies on nearly every side. God gave David victory in battle after battle, at a terrible price in human lives. Then when the kingdom seemed secure, David had a love affair with the wife of one of his most trusted soldiers, Uriah the Hittite. The woman became pregnant. David arranged for Uriah to die in battle, so he could marry the mother of his illegitimate son.

Yes, David had plenty of grief in his life. We see it surface again and again in the Psalms. The child born of David's adultery was stricken with a serious illness, and David wept before the Lord (see 2 Sam. 12:15–23). He fasted and prayed, pleading that the baby would be spared. Scholars believe that during this time he wrote Psalm 51, which says:

> Have mercy on me, O God,
>   according to thy steadfast love;
> according to thy abundant mercy
>   blot out my transgressions.
> Wash me thoroughly from my iniquity,
>   and cleanse me from my sin!
> (vv. 1,2 RSV).

This is the cry of a grieving heart, a cry of confession and repentance. David knew he had done wrong, and he prayed that the Lord would not hold it against his family. But in seven days the child died. "Then David arose from the earth, and washed, and anointed himself, and changed his apparel, and came into the house of the LORD, and worshipped," the Bible says. "Then he came to his own house; and when he required, they set bread before him, and he did eat" (2 Sam. 12:20).

David's servants were puzzled. Why had he stopped mourning? While the child was sick, David had poured out his sorrow to the Lord; shouldn't he be more sorrowful, now that the child was dead?

David disagreed. ". . . While the child was yet alive, I fasted and wept: for I said, Who can tell whether GOD will be gracious to me, that the child may live? But now he is dead, wherefore should I fast? can I bring him back again? I shall go to him, but he shall not return to me" (vv. 22,23).

David showed great wisdom in the way he handled his grief. While the child suffered, he channeled his grief into prayer, pleading with the Lord. But when the child was dead, he got up and comforted his wife (v. 24). David did not wallow in grief; he did not let it get the best of him. Rather, he made the best of it.

Yet that was not the end of his sorrow. One of David's sons, Absalom, murdered his half-brother Amnon and fled to the region of Geshur. David grieved for Amnon. But finally he was able to put that sorrow behind him: "And the soul of king David longed to go forth unto Absalom: for he was comforted concerning Amnon, seeing he was dead" (2 Sam. 13:39).

Absalom did return to his father, but soon plotted a revolt to take the kingdom by force. He tricked fifty of the king's choice warriors into making a pilgrimage to Hebron with him, then proclaimed himself king. Civil war broke out. David had to flee from his capital of Jerusalem and wage battle against his own son. He regained the city, but the war raged on for months. I can imagine David looking over the battlements, wringing his hands and pacing back and forth as he awaited the news of the battle. At last they came with the news that Absalom was dead. "And the king was much moved, and went up to the chamber over the gate, and wept: and as he went, thus he said, O my son Absalom, my son, my son Absalom! would God I had died for thee, O Absalom, my son, my son!" (2 Sam. 18:33).

David shut himself in a closet to mourn. His warriors returned from battle and David did not go out to meet them. He was grieving over their enemy! His chief of staff Joab barged into the king's room and said, ". . . Thou hast shamed this day the faces of all thy servants, which this day have saved thy life. . . ; In that thou lovest thine enemies, and hatest thy friends" (2 Sam. 19:5,6). His words were like daggers in David's bleeding heart. But David knew Joab was right. He got up and went to the balcony to welcome his soldiers home.

THE WIDOW OF NAIN

Now let us consider a New Testament example of grief. A widow in the little Judean city of Nain saw her only son die. We twentieth-century Americans could hardly imagine what a blow this must have been; we have Social Security, pensions, and food stamps to provide for someone in this predicament. There were no such things in those days. An older woman relied on her husband for income, and when he died, she depended on her son. This woman had lost both husband and son. She had to deal with the sorrow of death, but also with the awesome prospect of possible starvation.

The people of Nain felt sorry for the poor widow and filed out to join the funeral procession for her son. At that moment, Jesus arrived at the city gate. He saw the sad plight of the woman and came to offer His help. He walked up to the widow and said, "Weep not" (Luke 7:13).

If you or I were to walk up to a grieving friend in a funeral home and say, "Weep not," people would think we were heartless. Why should we cut off the natural flow of grief? Why should we refuse that mourner a time to express sorrow? But the Bible says that Jesus "taught them as one having authority" (Matt. 7:29). When He told the widow to stop crying she sensed there was a good reason for it. Jesus touched the funeral bier and halted the pallbearers. Again, this would be strange for anyone else to do, because the Jews' ceremonial law stated that a man who touched a funeral bier could not enter the synagogue until he had purified himself. Jesus paid no heed to that, even though the people expected Him to teach in the synagogue. Obviously, He knew something the people did not know.

Then the miracle. Jesus said, "Young man, I say unto thee, Arise" (Luke 7:14). The corpse came back to life. The young man sat up and looked around. Jesus presented him to his mother, alive and well once again.

What do you suppose would have happened if the widow had rejected Jesus? What if she had pushed Him aside when He told her to "weep not"? Would her son have been restored?

I think not. Scripture says that Jesus did not perform many miracles in His home town of Nazareth "because of their unbelief" (Matt. 13:58), and I suspect that the widow's unbelief would have hindered Him here. In her hour of sorrow, the widow of Nain was open to God; she was ready to receive His blessing, even though no blessing seemed possible. This is a vital lesson for anyone in a time of grief. Again quoting Matthew Henry:

> . . . Christ has concern for the mourners, for the miserable, and often goes before them with the blessings of his goodness. He undertook the work of our redemption and salvation, in his love and in his pity (Is. 63:9). Let poor widows comfort themselves that Christ pities them, and knows their sorrows; if others despise their grief, he does not.[2]

MARTHA AND MARY

Another poignant episode from the New Testament shows how two sisters, Martha and Mary, dealt with grief. This story is so full of meaning that John devotes an entire chapter of his Gospel to it (chap. 11).

Lazarus, Mary, and Martha lived in the village of Bethany, not far from Jerusalem. Jesus was a close friend of Lazarus, and we are sure that He visited many times in their home, which was like a hospitality station for the Master and His disciples on their frequent trips to the capital. One day Jesus received word that Lazarus was sick and that the sisters wanted Him to come. Yet Jesus seemed in no hurry to go. "This sickness is not unto death," He said, "but for the glory of God, that the Son of God might be glorified thereby" (John 11:4). He lingered two days on the other side of the Jordan River before making the trip to Bethany.

If only we could grasp this truth about every grief that comes our way! If only we could write across the obituary page, "This is for the glory of God, that the Son of God might be glorified!" If only we could say when we lie in a sickbed, "This is for the glory of God, that the Son of God might be glorified!" Such faith would transform our understanding of trouble. It would revolutionize our attitude toward pain and death.

C. S. Lewis said that we self-assured human beings often consider God to be an "interruption" to our lives. We think we have all that we need, even though that "all" does not include the Creator. So God must speak through pain and suffering to catch our attention, to remind us that we depend upon Him for life and health. Pain can be "God's megaphone"[3] to call us back to Him. In this case, I don't think Lazarus or his sisters needed the amplification of "God's megaphone"; but their friends and neighbors did. So God was willing to let Lazarus die. He knew that he could use Lazarus' death to bring glory to Jesus, His Son. Could it be that he wants to use your grief in the same way?

At last Jesus came to Bethany. Even before he met the two sisters, He knew that Lazarus was dead (11:14). He knew. Martha ran out to meet Him and said, "Lord, if thou hadst been here, my brother had not died" (v. 21). Grieving people may be tempted to think this. They say, "I must not be close enough to the Lord or this thing wouldn't have happened to me." That's not necessarily so. Jesus does not give you a blanket insurance policy against trouble. In fact, He may let the trouble come so that He can be glorified through it, honored by the way you respond.

Martha bore that out. She said, ". . . I know that even now, whatsoever thou wilt ask of God, God will give it thee" (v. 22). She had faith in the Lord Jesus, despite her grief. She knew He would give her what was best in this situation, so she turned herself over to Him. She trusted Him.

Jesus promised Martha that Lazarus would rise from the dead. At first she had trouble understanding this; she did not realize what He was offering to do. Then Mary came and threw herself at Jesus' feet, weeping. Her friends milled about, weeping and wailing for her dead brother. It was a pitiful sight, and the Bible says Jesus "groaned in the spirit, and was troubled" (v. 33). If your heart is full of grief, think of this: Jesus is groaning with you. He feels the sorrow you feel. He's right there beside you, crying all the while. He knows your grief.

While he was yet in tears, Jesus went to Lazarus' tomb and asked bystanders to remove the stone that sealed the door. Then He lifted up his eyes to heaven and called upon God to raise Lazarus from the dead. He shouted into the dark recesses of the tomb, "Lazarus, come forth!" (v. 43).

And the once dead Lazarus came out of the tomb, still wearing the grave clothes. Jesus told the astonished crowd to unwrap him and let him go.

THE MIRACLE OF GRIEF

These two cases of grief from the New Testament—concerning the widow of Nain and Lazarus' sisters—are bound to make someone ask, "Why doesn't God bring my loved one back to life?" Or, "Why doesn't He work a miracle to solve my problem?" To our human minds, this seems like the best way to solve our grief: Ask God to take away the reason for the grief. Have Him bring the dead back to life or restore the deranged mind or wipe out the terrible crime we have committed. That seems like the best solution. Sometimes God does work a miracle that way. But more often He works the *miracle of grief.*

What do I mean by that? I mean that when you are able to accept your grief and rise above it through the power of God, that is as great a miracle—perhaps more of a miracle—than if God removed the problem. When you affirm that Jesus loves you in spite of your suffering, that is a miracle. When you confess that God knows what is best for you, even though you can't see why He lets you suffer, that is a miracle. You may not realize this until you endure grief yourself. But thousands of Christians know it is true.

Dr. Franklin Miller suffered a wearisome string of ailments: a massive heart attack, gall bladder disease, cancer of the prostate gland. Yet each new disorder introduced him to a deeper level of faith. He writes:

> Gratitude continues to overwhelm me for God's goodness and graciousness toward me. I no longer worry about many of the problems of life but approach those problem areas with confidence that Christ will be present and direct me, that His glorious love and mercy might be shown to a world suffering with sickness, tragedy, and death. My fear of death is much relieved. Now I experience more strongly the will to live, not only on this earth but through eternity, for I have found in Him life abundant.[4]

Looking back on my own experience, I know that I might not have entered the ministry if God had not allowed me to suffer tuberculosis. I could see no value in that illness at the time. I could not imagine that God would use it to put my life on the right course, but He did. My calling proved once again the truth of Romans 8:28: "And we know that all things work together for good to them that love God, to them who are the called according to his purpose."

Have you lost your husband or wife to death? God will make something good of that heartache . . .

Are you suffering a terminal disease? God will make something good of that pain . . .

Have your children left home with a vicious, rebellious attitude? God will make something good of that anguish . . .

Does your boss seem to criticize everything you do, no matter how hard you try? God will make something good of that hurt . . .

. . . *if* you are called according to His purpose. That's the key. You may never see any good come out of these situations if you turn away from God. But if you surrender your life to Him and live obediently as His child, the promise of Romans 8:28 belongs to you. The Bible assures us, ". . . There hath not failed one word of all his good promise . . ." (1 Kin. 8:56). "Heaven and earth shall pass away, but my words shall not pass away" (Matt. 24:35).

The experiences of people in the Bible prove over and over: Give your grief to God, and He will make a miracle.

NOTES

1. Matthew Henry and Thomas Scott, *Commentary on the Holy Bible*, Vol. I (Nashville: Thomas Nelson Publishers, 1979), p. 13.
2. Ibid., Vol. III, p. 245.
3. C. S. Lewis, *The Problem of Pain* (New York: Macmillan Company, 1962), pp. 95,96.
4. Quoted by Kenneth E. Schemmer, *Between Faith and Tears* (Nashville: Thomas Nelson Publishers, 1981), p. 118.

8

ARE YOU READY FOR THIS?

A friend prods your ribs to get your attention. "Are you ready for this?" he snickers. You know he has a joke to tell and, ready or not, here it comes!

Often life does much the same thing. When we least expect it, an illness or an accident surprises us. The voice of tragedy asks, "Are you ready for this?"

But grief is no joke.

My sister Leona was pastor of a church in Baton Rouge, Louisiana, when she noticed some unusual symptoms of illness. She experienced sudden fainting spells. Her vision blurred. Muscles twitched uncontrollably. She lost control of her extremities; one by one, her fingers refused to obey the brain's commands, then her wrists went limp. Chewing and swallowing became difficult. During this time, she felt excruciating pain throughout her body.

Leona asked several ministers to pray for her healing, but she progressively worsened. She visited a series of nine medical specialists for diagnosis. Their verdict was unanimous: muscular dystrophy!

One of the doctors took Leona's gnarled hand and gently said, "So young. So very young."

"You'll need a wheelchair soon," said another.

Her weight had dwindled to eighty-eight pounds and she could scarcely keep her balance. Often she fell down stairs and badly bruised herself. She writes:

I had always been so strong—seemed as though I had the

strength of six people. Now, crippled, weakened, and in constant pain, I could no longer perform many of the daily tasks one must do—like combing my hair, cleaning the house, or the simple act of turning a knob on the door. If I were outside and wanted in, I had to wait until someone heard my thumping and opened the door. . . .

My dreams lay shattered at my feet. All hope of restored health was gone. . . .[1]

What would you do in this situation? Where would you turn for help? Would you be ready to cope with the stress of such a tragedy?

In Leona's case, she held onto the Lord and trusted Him to heal her, even though her doctors had given up hope. She believed the promise of healing that she found in God's Word. In the end, God did heal her body and restored her to an active ministry. She and the man she married, the Rev. James Murphy, are now part of our staff at LeSea. But not everyone responds this way. Some get angry with God when tragedy comes into their lives. Their faith is not strong enough to make them shockproof against tragedy.

Let's look at the experiences of several people—some in the Bible and some in more recent times—who had to deal with personal tragedy. Let's see what we can learn from them.

ABRAHAM

Abraham was born in the Mesopotamian city of Ur sometime around 2000 B.C. He went with his father Terah and their family to the city of Haran, where Terah died. Then God told Abraham (or "Abram" as he was called then) to leave Haran and travel farther west, "unto a land that I will shew thee" (Gen. 12:1). He promised to make of Abraham's descendants "a great nation" (v. 2) that would carry His blessing to the far corners of the earth.

Abraham obeyed the Lord. He led his family on a long and eventful journey through what is now Palestine, the Sinai, Egypt, and then back to Palestine. By that time, Abraham was in his eighties. And he said, ". . . Lord GOD, what wilt thou give me, seeing I go childless . . . ?" (Gen. 15:2).

Instead of a gift, God renewed His promise to Abraham. He said he would make Abraham's descendants more numerous than the stars of heaven (Gen. 15:5).

More years passed with no children. Abraham was ninety-nine years old. God appeared to him again and repeated that He would make the man's descendants "exceeding fruitful" (Gen. 17:6). Abraham's aged wife Sarah conceived and bore a son, whom they named *Isaac*, meaning "laughter" (because Sarah thought it funny that she should bear a child in her old age). *At last,* Abraham must have thought, *I have seen my mission fulfilled.*

Then, while Isaac was still a boy, God told Abraham to sacrifice him on Mount Moriah (Gen. 22:1,2).

The Bible does not say whether Abraham complained or questioned God, but I am sure this sudden change of plans must have made him wonder. Why would God want to cut off his descendants? Why promise him prosperity and blessing, only to let him down at the end of his life? This quick, unexplained demand of God must have struck a tragic blow to Abraham's heart. ". . . Abraham had to cut himself off from his entire past when he left his homeland and now was summoned to give up his entire future."[2] Yet Abraham saddled up his donkey and set off for Mount Moriah to obey.

Moriah is the highest of the hills where Jerusalem is now located. The Islamic Mosque of Omar today stands over the rock where Abraham is supposed to have taken Isaac for the sacrifice. I have visited that mosque on several occasions, and I can just imagine the rough, weatherbeaten old man trudging up the hillside to offer his son on that craggy platform of stone. I can picture the intense agony on Abraham's face as they neared the place of sacrifice with a bundle of sticks tied to the donkeys back. Young Isaac wondered where they were going to get the sacrifice; he had seen his father offer animal sacrifices before, and he expected this to be the same.

Abraham piled up stones for the altar. He arranged the sticks on top of it. He lit the wood and watched the flames roar high. Then he quickly seized his son, tied the boy's hands behind him, and raised his dagger to cut Isaac's throat. I can imagine the old man thought, *Lord, I don't know how you will do it, but I know You will give me a son yet. Even though Isaac goes down into the ashes, You can raise him up. I know You won't fail Your promise.*

But God stayed Abraham's knife. He kept him from killing the boy. Abraham's faith had been tested and proven strong. At that very moment, he heard a ram caught in a thicket and God revealed that this animal would take Isaac's place (Gen. 22:13).

When tragedy came to Abraham, he obeyed and trusted God for the outcome.

BLIND BARTIMAEUS

A blind man named Bartimaeus lived in the town of Jericho. Each day he groped his way down to the main thoroughfare, where he squatted to beg from the passersby. If you have ever visited the Middle East, you know the squalid life these beggars have. Bare tatters of clothing hang on their backs, flies swarm around their faces, their bones protrude from hunger. Most people turn to the other side of the street, just to avoid passing near them.

One day Bartimaeus heard a noisy crowd coming down the street. He wondered if perhaps the Roman governor or some other dignitary were coming his way.

"Who's coming?" he asked the people who brushed past him.

"Jesus of Nazareth," they said. "Jesus is passing this way."

No doubt Bartimaeus had heard about Jesus. The Bible says His reputation had been spread throughout the land. Bartimaeus probably knew that Jesus healed people and raised them from the dead and taught with great authority. In every way, He seemed to be the Messiah the Jews had prayed for so long. But Jesus did not plan to stop at Bartimaeus' town. He was simply "passing this way." Apparently Bartimaeus would miss his only chance to be healed.

The blind man got to his feet and squeezed into the midst of the crowd. "Jesus, Son of David," he shouted, "have mercy on me!" (Luke 18:38 NKJB–NT).

The curious throng tried to push him back. "Be quiet, old fellow," one of them snarled. "Jesus has no time for you!"

But Bartimaeus pushed harder and cried out all the more. "Son of David, have mercy on me!"

Jesus heard him. He stopped. "Bring that man to Me," the Master said.

When the crowd pulled back to allow Bartimaeus to come through, Jesus said, "What do you want Me to do for you?" (v. 41 NKJB–NT).

Notice Bartimaeus' reply. When people are hit by tragedy, their first plea may be, "Lord, ease the pain," or "Lord, don't let me suffer long," or something to that effect. They don't trust God for a remedy; they trust Him just enough for temporary relief. Bartimaeus had more faith than that. He said, "Lord, I want to receive my sight."

So that's exactly what the Lord gave him. He said, "Receive your sight; your faith has saved you" (v. 42 NKJB–NT). Bartimaeus immediately was able to see.

When tragedy came to Bartimaeus, he asked Jesus for deliverance—and Jesus provided mightily.

JOHN BUNYAN

Born in 1628 in the village of Bedford, England, the son of a tinsmith, John Bunyan trained to take up his father's trade until the English Civil War drew him into the military. During the war, he felt the Lord convicting him to become a Christian. So he accepted the Lord and started preaching for the Nonconformist Church, which had broken away from the Church of England. His preaching and tract-writing landed Bunyan in prison again and again, but each time he was released, he went back to his ministry.

Bunyan never knew when the king's guard would knock on his door and hustle him off to prison. Talk about tragedy—for Bunyan, tragedy became a way of life. I have visited Bedford Jail and seen the tiny stone window where his wife delivered his meals. We modern tourists cannot conceive of the brutal conditions he must have suffered in that dank, musty place. One biographer writes:

> . . . Parted from his wife and children, for whose welfare he suffered painful anxiety, he was confined in what was indeed a "den"—a breeding-place of jail-fever. There was no chimney in it, and we have to think of him as sleeping on straw. Yet . . . opportunities for the exercise of his vocation were not lacking in prison, and he took them assiduously. Moreover, he wrote immensely, and his themes, as we can see from the great body of his writings, were those of his preaching. . . .[3]

Bunyan took advantage of his long prison terms to write tracts, sermons, and inspirational books for the world outside. It probably was during one of these prison stays that he began *The Pilgrim's Progress,* one of the greatest Christian devotional books ever written.

When tragedy came to John Bunyan, he focused on God and made the most of what he had.

ALEXANDER SOLZHENITSYN

The Russian Christian, Alexander Solzhenitsyn, whom I mentioned earlier, is a modern example of how a person can respond to tragedy in a healthy, constructive way. Born in 1918, Solzhenitsyn was a child during the early days of the Communist Revolution in Russia. By the time Joseph Stalin came to power, he was studying mathematics and physics at a local university. Solzhenitsyn's keen, analytical mind also studied the government of Russia and turned up some very disturbing questions. Why did so many men on Stalin's staff die suddenly and mysteriously? Why did so many Russian laborers suffer under Stalin's "progressive" regime? Why was decision-making power concentrated in the hands of fewer and fewer people, instead of being spread out, as Lenin predicted it would be?

Solzhenitsyn's studies were interrupted by World War II, when he was drafted into the Russian Army. As an artillery officer, he was decorated for bravery with the Order of the Red Star. However, Solzhenitsyn still felt uncomfortable with his government; he exchanged letters with a friend, criticizing Stalin. These letters fell into the government's hands, and Solzhenitsyn was arrested. The arresting officers stripped him of rank and medals and sent him to a slave labor camp.

To make matters worse, Solzhenitsyn developed abdominal cancer in the labor camp. The camp doctors performed surgery, but the cancer continued to spread. He was sent to a hospital at Tashkent, where doctors gave him massive doses of X-ray, enough to kill a man. Solzhenitsyn became a "guinea pig" for their experiments.

Only his faith in God brought him through this suffering. Solzhenitsyn is a devout Russian Orthodox Christian, and he prayed that God would deliver him from the double bondage of

131

cancer and imprisonment. Later he committed one of these prayers to paper:

> *How easy it is for me to live with you, Lord!*
> *How easy it is for me to believe in you.*
> *When my spirit is lost, perplexed, and cast down,*
> *When the sharpest can see no further than the night,*
> *And know not what on the morrow they must do*
> *You give me a sure certainty*
> *That you exist, that you are watching over me. . . .*[4]

God worked a miracle. The cancer went into remission. In 1956, Solzhenitsyn was permitted to move to a camp near Moscow, where he saw his wife for the first time since 1942. Gradually, the Soviet government gave him more freedom, and Solzhenitsyn began writing stories about his experiences in the labor camp. Premier Nikita Krushchev was anxious to dispel the saintly image of Stalin, so Solzhenitsyn's accounts of the brutal treatment under Stalin won ready acclaim. Krushchev hosted him at a gala ball for Soviet authors and artists. He won the Nobel Prize for Literature in 1970. But by that time, his criticism had turned towards Krushchev's regime as well, and Solzhenitsyn was considered an enemy of the state. The last straw was Solzhenitsyn's prizewinning novel, *The First Circle*, a tale of life among a group of scientists in one of Stalin's labor camps. As one reviewer noted, "Solzhenitsyn makes clear that the prison is a small-scale model of all Russia and that the prisoners, guards, and overseers are all in the same hell together."[5]

Without his world fame, Solzhenitsyn might have been exiled to the prison camps again. Since that would have been too embarrassing, the Soviet government had no choice: They could only expel him from Russia.

In every tragic situation, Solzhenitsyn has learned to adjust and accept the new role God has given him. He can echo Paul's words: ". . . For I have learned, in whatsoever state I am, therewith to be content. I know both how to be abased, and I know how to abound: . . . both to be full and to be hungry, both to abound and to suffer need. I can do all things through Christ which strengtheneth me" (Phil. 4:11–13).

When tragedy came to Solzhenitsyn, he learned to be content.

"READY TO DO THY WILL"

Tragedy is an unexpected turn in the course of life. If you are not ready for it, tragedy can knock you flat, so you must prepare for it. You must expect the unexpected, knowing that God can guide your life even then. A. C. Palmer wrote a precious hymn that sums it up well:

> *Ready to suffer grief or pain,*
> *Ready to stand the test;*
> *Ready to stay at home and send*
> *Others if He sees best.*

> *Ready to speak, ready to warn,*
> *Ready o'er souls to yearn;*
> *Ready in life, ready in death,*
> *Ready for His return.*

Chorus

> *Ready to go, ready to stay,*
> *Ready my place to fill;*
> *Ready for service, lowly or great,*
> *Ready to do His will.*[6]

How about you? Are you ready for whatever this day brings—even if it brings tragedy?

NOTES

1. Leona Sumrall Murphy, "Healed of Muscular Dystrophy," *World Harvest,* Sept./Oct. 1978, p. 13.
2. Charles M. Laymon, ed., *The Interpreter's One-Volume Commentary on the Bible* (Nashville: Abingdon Press, 1971), p. 18.
3. From an afterword by T. R. Lewis in John Bunyan, *The Pilgrim's Progress* (New York: Signet Classics, 1964), p. 291.
4. Quoted by Niels C. Nielson, Jr., *Solzhenitsyn's Religion* (Nashville: Thomas Nelson Publishers, 1975), pp. 9,10.
5. Seymour Kurtz, ed., *The New York Times Encyclopedic Almanac: 1970* (New York: The New York Times, 1969), p. 636.
6. *Hymns of the Christian Life,* rev. ed. (Harrisburg, Pa.: Christian Publications, Inc., 1962), number 440.

9

HE'S ACQUAINTED WITH GRIEF

The woman took nearly an hour to pour out her story of grief. She was suffering an illness that doctors could not diagnose; her family turned a deaf ear to her complaints; her fellow workers thought she was a hypochondriac. Her situation was sad indeed.

Finally the pastor spoke. He began to tell her about the love of Jesus Christ and how she needed to yield her life completely to Him.

"Oh, pastor," she interrupted. "You just don't understand!"

"Perhaps I don't," the pastor smiled. "But let me introduce you to Someone who does."

I am convinced that Jesus Christ is the answer to your grief, too. In the previous chapters, I have tried to help you understand what grief is and what it can do to your life. I have suggested how you can counteract the deadly effects of grief, whether or not you are a Christian. But I would not be fair to you or faithful to the truth, if I closed this book without showing you the ultimate answer to your grief.

YOU NEED HELP

We have seen that the causes of grief are many. Grief can be brought about through neglect of or reckless disregard for yourself. If you start drinking alcohol, you will come to grief. If you start using tobacco, you will come to grief. If you depend on drugs to pep you up, calm you down, or steady your nerves, you will come to grief. On the other hand, grief can come through no fault of your own; it may be unavoidable. Auto accidents, tornadoes, heart attacks, and other kinds of tragedy—these are not necessarily a consequence of past actions, but they will affect your life forever.

No matter what the cause of grief, one aspect of the plight is certain: When grief comes, you will need help.

You may not find help where you first look. You may try to dance your grief away on the dance floor or dispel those feelings of despair with an exotic vacation. You may try to distract yourself from grief by getting a second job. But entertainment or work cannot erase the grief. In the last few moments before you drift off to sleep at night, the grief comes back to haunt you. You know it still is festering in your soul.

You may go to physicians or psychologists for relief. They may be able to give you some help. Modern medicine can do wonders, and new counseling techniques can unlock deep dungeons of despair. But doctors and counselors can deal with only part of your problem. You are a three-room house with a body, soul, and spirit; any remedy that deals with only one or two sections of that "house" is just a partial remedy. It cannot get rid of all the grief.

So where do you turn for help? Who can help you carry the burden of grief?

SURELY HE KNOWS

Get a Bible and turn to Isaiah 53:3,4. This text is part of Isaiah's prophecy about the Messiah, the One who would come to save the world from sin. Notice what he says about the Savior:

> He is despised and rejected of men; a man of sorrows, and acquainted with grief: and we hid as it were our faces from him; he was despised, and we esteemed him not. Surely he hath borne our griefs, and carried our sorrows: yet we did esteem him stricken, smitten of God, and afflicted.

136

No matter how serious the grief that comes into your life, the Savior knows what it's like. Jesus Christ has suffered, too. He's been rejected, too. He understands your struggle and is ready to help you. He knows grief from His own experience. Examine that prophecy more closely:

"He is despised and rejected of men . . ." One of the most agonizing forms of grief is the grief of rejection. Two Japanese women once came to my study and told me how their husbands had rejected them. They had married GI's during World War II, but after returning to the States these men had left them to marry American women. Now, these women did not know what to do.

"Well, why not go back to Japan?" I said. "You know the way of life there. Your families are back there."

"Oh, Brother Sumrall, you do not understand," one of them sobbed. "We cannot go back. We have children, and in Japan they would be mongrels. Even the children in school would persecute them, say they were 'half-breeds.' They would never be happy there."

Rejection is a terrible thing. Yet in every country of the world, you will find some people rejected because of the color of their skin or some other feature that sets them apart. The grief of rejection is very common.

Jesus' own people rejected Him. The Jews despised Him because He did not lead His nation in the great revolution they expected the Messiah to bring. "He was in the world, and the world was made by him, and the world knew him not. He came unto his own, and his own received him not" (John 1:10,11). That rejection finally nailed Him to the cross. ". . . He was led as a sheep to the slaughter; and like a lamb dumb before his shearer, so opened he not his mouth" (Acts 8:32). Even with the prejudice of His own people against Him, Jesus did not complain. He did not protest the injustice of it all. He accepted what God had given Him to do, no matter what it brought.

". . . A man of sorrows . . ." I do not know anyone who has had more reason for sorrow than Jesus had. He was born in a dirty stable. While he was still an infant, his parents were forced to flee to a foreign land. He was misunderstood, ridiculed, and roughed up at every step of His ministry. He was betrayed by one of His closest friends. He was left to die between two wretched thieves. Yet despite all the sorrow in Jesus' life, He kept on loving people. Even when the Roman soldiers pounded the nails into His hands, He prayed that God would forgive them. He conquered the grief of sorrow.

While I was still a young preacher, I conducted a two-week series of meetings in Tennessee. After the second or third night, the pastor of this church took me aside and said, "We must close the meeting this Sunday."

"Why?" I asked. "Aren't the services going well?"

"Oh, the meetings are great," the pastor said. "You're a good evangelist. But my head deacon doesn't like you."

"Why not?"

"He didn't say. But he runs this church, and he told me to close the meetings Sunday night. I'm sorry."

I went back to my room and collapsed on the bed. I had nowhere to go, nothing scheduled for another week. And the meetings were going so well! What could I do? I felt such a heavy load of grief that I knelt down and started to pray about the problem.

"Lord, what shall I do?" I asked. "I've just tried to preach the gospel, and now I've been told to leave. How do You want me to handle this?"

The Lord said, "In tomorrow night's service, I want you to go to that deacon, hug him, and kiss him."

"Just a minute . . ." I said.

"Hug him and kiss him."

I must admit the Lord's answer was hard for me to accept. But at the next night's meeting, I asked the pastor to point out the deacon. He was a thin, wizened fellow, and when I embraced him I felt like I was hugging a telephone pole. "Brother, I love you!" I said.

The man said nothing.

That night I went back to my room and prayed again. "Lord, it didn't work," I said. "I got no response. What do You want me to do?"

"Kiss him again."

So the next night I walked up to the head deacon and gave him another big hug, kissed his cheek, and said, "I love you!"

The deacon said, "Ugh!" (I guess I squeezed too tight.)

"Lord, what now?" I prayed. "How can I get through to this man?"

"Do it again," the Lord said. "Hug and kiss him again."

So the third night I walked across the room, hugged the deacon again, and said, "Brother, I love you! God told me to say it."

He said, "I love you, too."

Thank God forever!

The man confessed that he did not like me because he thought I dressed too well, spoke too strongly, and was too sure of myself when I gave the altar call. That was only his opinion; if he had known how scared I was, preaching night after night in the only good suit I had, he would not have been offended.

On Sunday night, the pastor said, "Brother Sumrall, could you stay on for another week? Maybe longer?"

"But you said I would have to close."

"No, we don't want you to close," he said.

"You said your deacon wanted me to leave."

"He's changed his mind. You know what he said tonight? He said that was the best service he's ever attended, and he loves you more than any evangelist we've ever had."

My soul was bubbling over with joy. I could hear the Lord say, "See what three kisses can do?"

That's the kind of love Jesus had for His tormentors. Even in the depths of His sorrows, He loved people. In the depth of your sorrow, He'll show you how to love.

"*. . . Acquainted with grief. . .*" If you have never wrestled with grief, you'll have a hard time trying to comfort someone who is grieving. As the lady told her pastor, you "just don't understand" what that person is going through. This is why I thank God for the grief that has entered my life. I thank Him for the tuberculosis that nearly killed me. I thank Him for that sour deacon in Tennessee. I thank Him for the plane crash that killed my five friends. I thank Him because He used those experiences to teach me about grief.

The same was true of Jesus when He walked this earth. He experienced grief, day after day, so He knew how to talk with others about grief.

He looked upon the hungry multitude and said, "I have compassion on the multitude . . . and I will not send them away fasting, lest they faint in the way" (Matt. 15:32). So He performed a miracle, multiplying a few fish and loaves of bread to feed them all.

On another occasion, the Pharisees brought a woman they had caught in the act of adultery and asked what He thought they should do to her (John 8:1–11). They pointed out that the Law of Moses would put such a woman to death, and they were ready to stone her. Would the compassionate Jesus stop them? Would He violate God's Word? Jesus could see the deep sadness in the woman's eyes; He knew the guilt she carried because of her sin. He did not need to accuse her. He stooped and wrote in the sand. The Pharisees pressed Him for a decision, so He straightened up and said, "He that is without sin among you, let him first cast a stone at her" (v. 7). The Pharisees looked at one another. No one moved. But Jesus understood the situation very well; He knew that all of them were guilty of sin. In a moment,

He heard the *thump! thump! thump!* of stones being dropped to the ground. The Pharisees walked away.

Jesus said, "Woman, where are those thine accusers? hath no man condemned thee?"

She said, "No man, Lord."

"Neither do I condemn thee," Jesus said. "Go, and sin no more" (vv. 10,11).

Her grief was gone. She was forgiven, all because Jesus understood and picked up her load of grief.

Jesus crossed the Sea of Galilee to the region of Gadara, where a demon-possessed man fell at His feet and worshiped Him (Mark 5:1–20). I have prayed with hundreds of demon-possessed people, and I know they are full of grief. Their lives are wracked with torment. Jesus saw that in this man's life. He cast the demons out of the man, and the demoniac returned to his right mind. He asked Jesus if he could join His disciples.

But Jesus said, "Go home to thy friends, and tell them how great things the Lord hath done for thee, and hath had compassion on thee" (v. 19).

Jesus has compassion on grief-stricken people. He picks up the burden of grief. Even though He's well acquainted with grief, He does not fear it. He knows He can conquer it.

". . . *Surely he hath borne our griefs and carried our sorrows. . . .*" That's a wonderful thing to know, isn't it? We don't need to carry our grief alone. We don't have to struggle under the burden of sorrow, pain, and doubt. Jesus offers to be our Burden-bearer and Sorrow-sharer.

Every Sunday at the altar of Christian Center Church in South Bend, I pray with people who have not allowed the Lord to carry their burdens. They have tried to do it on their own. They have fumbled with their grief—and failed. As a last resort, they come to the altar and turn it over to the Lord. He delivers them from grief and gives them victory over the problems that trouble them.

How much better their lives would be if they had discovered this sooner! How much better *your* life would be if you could let go of the grief you are carrying! Let me offer a prayer for you:

Dear Jesus, I thank You for the privilege of sharing the truth about grief with the person who holds this book. I do not know this person by name, but You do. Search this person's life right now and see if he harbors any grief:
—A fear of the unknown
—A sorrow over death
—A bitter attitude toward someone
—A wasted life.
Lord, whatever causes anguish of soul for this person, I pray that you will bring it to light. Name this burden for what it is. Help this person to surrender it to You.

And then, dear Jesus, I pray that you will fill this person's life with unspeakable joy and "the peace that passes understanding"—the peace that comes only from surrendering his life to you. Then I know that this person will be truly blessed, and we will give You all the praise. Amen.

If this study has helped to break the power of grief in your life, write me and tell me about it. I will rejoice with you. I stand ready to help you in any way I can. My address is:

Lester Sumrall
Box 12
South Bend, Indiana 46614